Chinese Diet Therapy

China Esperanto Press

Beijing   1996

First Edition 1996

Compiled by Zhao Muying
Translated by Wen Jingen

ISBN 7 − 5052 − 0307 − X/G.84

Published by China Esperanto Press
P. O. Box 77, 24 Baiwanzhuang Rd. , Beijing 100037, China
Printed by Beijing Baihua Colour Printing Co. Ltd.
Distributed by China International Book Trading Corporation
35 Chegongzhuang Xilu, Beijing 100044, China
P. O. Box 399, Beijing, China

Printed in the People's Republic of China

Foreword

Ancient Chinese medical men believed that medicine and diet were one in the same thing. Some people put forward the principle that "the five cereals are used to provide nutrition; the five fruits, for secondary; the flesh of the five kinds of birds, for invigoration and the five vegetables, for replenishment and nutrition" (Here "five" means "plural", "many", "all kinds of", etc. — Translator). Man depends on these ordinary materials to sustain life generation after generation. The right diet not only nourishes and strengthens the body, but prevents diseases and prolongs life. Chinese people has arrived at various diet recipes through long practice and these recipes, collected and collated and developed by medical men, make part of the national legacy, which contributes much to the prosperity of the Chinese nation. Historical documents prove that diet therapy was widely applied among the ordinary people as well as in the imperial court in China as early as 2000 years ago. The earliest medical treatise on traditional Chines medicine, the *Yellow Emperor's Internal Classic* (*Huang Di Nei Jing*) contains records of medicated diet prescriptions. Medical men of later generations all paid full attention to this respect and they made their own contribution to developments in this field.

In recent years the rapid development of modern industry has caused a serious world-wide imbalance in the ecology, and this has aroused in people a strong desire to "return to nature", with people beginning to favor "green

1

food". The cure and prevention of some diseases by means of diet have become a general focus. Many medical researchers in China are exploring and researching literature on the diet therapy in traditional Chinese medicine, and collecting and collating effective folk prescriptions for a medicated diet. Some medical experts are publishing prescriptions from their own clinical experiences in diet therapy and others are publicizing secret prescriptions that have been handed down from their ancestors...

It is from thousands of recipes in works such as these that *Chinese Diet Therapy* has selected the 570 recipes included here, which cover 62 common diseases and syndromes. These prescriptions have definite curative effects and at the same time they are easy to process at home. Special remarks are made where some drugs are incompatible with certain other foods or drugs. The reader can choose the appropriate recipe in accordance with their illness, where they live and what is accessible to them.

Considering that English-speaking readers may not be familiar with some of the drugs described in this book, a glossary is attached at the end of the book where readers will find the Latin and Chinese equivolents of the drugs referred to herein.

Finally we would like to call our reader's attention to a very important point: **although diet therapy exerts positive curative effects in some aspects, medicine and other treatments must not be neglected**. Before you adopt any prescriptions from this book, you should have your disease carefully diagnosed by a doctor — only then can you make a right choice. If your case is serious or complicated, you must see a doctor in good time lest you let slip the opportunity for treatment at the earliest possible time.

Contents

4

7

Recipes for Dermatological Diseases ·················· 132

13

Recipes For Children's Diseases 165

14

Recipes for E.N.T. Diseases and Ophthalmological Diseases

15

16

Recipes for Internal Diseases

COLD AND INFLUENZA

Decoction of Ginger, Sugar and Tea

Ingredients:

Ginger	10 g
Tea	7 g
Brown sugar	15 g

Process and application:

Wash the ginger clean, decoct it with tea and dissolve brown sugar in the decoction. Take the decoction after meal.

Curative properties: Cold; cough; aversion to cold.

Decoction of Walnut, Bulb of Green Chinese Onion, Ginger and Tea

Ingredients:

Walnut	25 g
Bulb of green Chinese onion	25 g
Fresh ginger	25 g
Tea	15 g

Process and application:

Pound walnut, bulb of green Chinese onion and fresh ginger, put them with tea in an earthenware pot, add one and half bowls of water and decoct them. Strain off the liquid. Take all the decoction at a draft and lie under quilt, avoiding exposure to a draught.

Curative properties: Fever due to cold; headache and anhidrosis.

Parched Rice Gruel with Fresh Ginger

Ingredients:

Fresh ginger	30 g to 50 g
Parched rice	50 g

Process and application:

Cut fresh ginger into slices and cook them and the parched rice until they become gruel. Eat the gruel after seasoning it with a little table salt and peanut oil (with the fresh ginger slices or without them).

Curative properties: Nasal obstruction with running nose; cough with thin phlegm; anorexia etc.

Noodle with White Pepper

Ingredients:

White pepper	a little
Bulb of green Chinese onion	some

Process and application:

Prepare a bowl of noodle, put in bulb of green Chinese onion and white pepper and mix them well. Eat the noodle hot and lie under quilt. A curative effect will be felt when the patient perspires.

Curative properties: Cold.

Duck Egg White Soup

Ingredients:

Duck-egg whites	2
Bulbs of green Chinese onion	4

Brown sugar	50 g

Process and application:

Put the bulb of green Chinese onion, brown sugar and 2 teacups of water in a pot. Heat the pot until the water boils. Pour the hot liquid into a bowl with the duck-egg whites and stir it. Take the soup warm in 2 separate doses in one day. Sour, hot and stimulant food should be avoided.

Curative properties: Cough, hoarseness, guttural swelling pain due to cold.

Stewed Pig Heart with Salt

Ingredients:

Fresh pig heart	1
Table salt	some

Process and application:

Wash the pig heart clean and drain off the water. Put it into an iron pot with a little water and scatter table salt over the pig heart. Stew it over soft fire for about one hour. Shake off the salt from the pig heart and eat it hot, once or twice each day. The curative effect will be achieved after one or two doses have been taken.

Curative properties: Cough due to cold; cough due to bronchitis.

Soup of Root of Peking Cabbage with White Sugar

Ingredients:

Root of Peking cabbage	1
White sugar	some

Process and application:

Wash the root of Peking cabbage clean, chop it, put it and a bowlful of water in a pot and decoct it. Dissolve the white sugar in the soup. Take it twice a day.

Curative properties: Influenza.

Watermelon and Tomato Juice

Ingredients:

Watermelon	some
Tomato	some

Process and application:

Wrap seeded watermelon flesh in gauze and squeeze its juice out. Rinse the tomato in boiling water, peel and seed it and wrap it in gauze and squeeze its juice out. Combine the juices together for drinking.

Curative properties: Fever, thirst, dysphoria, burning sensation during dark urination due to cold in summer; anorexia, maldigestion etc.

Big White Radish Juice

Ingredients:

Big white radish	some

Process and application:

Wash the big white radish clean, smash it and extract its juice. Put drops of the juice into the nose, several times a day.

Curative properties: Headache due to cold, heatstroke or apoplexy.

Gruel with Bulb of Green Chinese Onion and Garlic

Ingredients:

Bulbs of green Chinese onion	10
Garlic	3
Glutinous rice	100 g

Process and application:

Prepare gruel with glutinous rice. When the gruel is cooked, put in the bulbs of green Chinese onion and garlic and continue boiling the gruel for a moment. Take all the gruel hot at a time and lie under quilt. A curative effect will be felt when the patient perspires.

Curative properties: Headache due to cold.

Fresh Garlic (for Sucking)

Ingredients:

Fresh garlic   3 cloves

Process and application:

Put a clove of fresh garlic in the mouth and keep it there. Swallow down the saliva if secreted. When it has become tasteless, spit it out and take another clove. A curative effect will be achieved when the 3 cloves have been all used.

Curative properties: Running nose at the first stage of cold.

Egg Soup with Fresh Ginger, Green Chinese Onion and Pear

Ingredients:

Pear	120 g
Fresh ginger	15 g
Bulb of green Chinese onion	15 g
Hen's eggs	2

Process and application:

Boil the pear, fresh ginger and bulb of green Chinese onion in water. Beat the eggs in a bowl, stir it thoroughly and pour in the boiled liquid and mix them well. Drink the soup hot and lie under quilt. A curative effect will be felt when the patient perspires.

Curative properties: Cold, cough.

Lichee Meat Stewed in Yellow Rice or Millet Wine

Ingredients:

Dried lichee meat	30 g
Yellow rice or millet wine	some

Process and application:

Stew the lichee meat in yellow rice or millet wine and take it hot at a draft.

Curative properties: Nasal obstruction due to cold.

Infusion of Green Tea and Mung Bean

Ingredients:

Mung bean	50 g
Green tea	5 g
Crystal sugar	15 g

Process and application:

Wash the mung bean clean, pound it, put it together with green tea and crystal sugar in a bowl and let them infuse in boiling water for 20 minutes. Take the infusion as a drink.

Curative properties: Influenza with complications of sore-throat, cough etc.

Apple and Raisin Gruel

Ingredients:

Apple	1
Raisins	30 g
Rice	100 g

Sugar   50 g
Process and application:
Cook thin gruel with rice, put in apple slices, raisins
and sugar and continue cooking the gruel for 5 minutes.
Take the gruel hot and lie under quilt. A curative effect
will be felt when the patient perspires.
Curative properties: Cold. (This therapy is especially
effective for aged people, children and women in childbirth.)

COUGH

Tea with Dried Tangerine Peel

Ingredients:
Tea   2 g
Dried tangerine peel   2 g
Brown sugar   30 g
Process and application:
Infuse the ingredients in hot water for 6 minutes.
Take one dose after lunch every day.
Curative properties: Cough.

White Spirit with "Snow Pear"

Ingredients:
"Snow pear" (*Pyrus serotina Rehd.*)   500 g
White spirit   1000 g
Process and application:
Wash the "snow pear" clean, peel it, decore it and
then cut it into 5-mm square cubes. Put the slices into a jar
with white spirit and seal the jar hermetically. Let the pear
soak in white spirit for 7 days and stir the white spirit every
third day. Drink as much as one feels fit.

Curative properties: Cough; constipation etc.

Glutinous Rice Gruel with Bulb of Green Chinese Onion

Ingredients:

Bulb of green Chinese onion	5 pcs (each in length of 3 cm)
Glutinous rice	60 g
Fresh ginger	5 slices
Rice vinegar	5 ml

Process and application:

Cook gruel with bulb of green Chinese onion and glutinous rice and add 5 ml of rice vinegar. Eat the gruel hot.

Curative properties: Early stage of cough with thin phlegm; headache and nasal obstruction.

Chinese-date, Brown Sugar and Pumpkin

Ingredients:

Pumpkin (peeled)	500 g
Chinese-dates(stoned)	12 - 20
Brown sugar	some

Process and application:

Cook the ingredients in water and eat them.

Curative properties: Cough due to senile chronic bronchitis

Peanuts and Crystal Sugar

Ingredients:

Shelled peanuts	100 - 150 g

Crystal sugar   some

Process and application:

Cook them in clear water. Eat the peanuts and drink the decoction.

Curative properties: Chronic bronchitis; dry cough with little phlegm.

Apricot Kernel Gruel

Ingredients:

Apricot kernel	20 g
Rice	100 g
White sugar	150 g

Process and application:

After soaking the apricot kernel in warm water, skin and pestle them. Grind the apricot kernel in 3000 ml of clear water and boil this liquid with washed rice till the rice is overdone. Put in sugar and mix it well with the gruel. Take the gruel warm in the morning and in the evening every day.

Curative properties: Cough due to cold; constipation etc.

Walnut Kernel Gruel

Ingredients:

Walnut kernel	100 g
Rice and white sugar	some for each

Process and application:

Pound the walnut kernel and wash the rice clean. Cook them in water until they become gruel. Eat the gruel after adding some sugar.

Curative properties: Cough; senile constipation.

Decoction of Radish and Bulb of Green Chinese Onion

Ingredients:

Radish	1
Bulbs of green Chinese onion	6
Fresh ginger	15 g

Process and application:

Decoct the radish in 3 bowlfuls of water until it is done. Put in the bulbs of green Chinese onion and fresh ginger and continue boiling it until one bowl of decoction is left. Take all the decoction together with the dregs at a time.

Curative properties: Cough with abundant expectoration.

Decoction of Fresh Ginger, Chinese-date and Brown Sugar

Ingredients:

Brown sugar	30 g
Fresh ginger	15 g
Chinese-date	30 g

Process and application:

Decoct the above ingredients in three bowlfuls of water. This decoction produces effect when the patient perspires a bit after eating it.

Curative properties: Cough due to cold; diarrhea after childbirth.

Horse Milk

Ingredients:

Fresh horse milk   300 ml
White sugar   some
Process and application:
Boil the horse milk and take it after adding some sugar
to it.
Curative properties: Cough due to pulmonary tuber-
culosis.

Radish and Pig's Lung

Ingredients:
Radish   1
Pig's lung   1
Apricot kernel   15 g
Process and application:
Decoct the above ingredients in water for one hour.
Eat the pig's lung together with the soup.
Curative properties: Persistent chronic cough.

White Sugar and Hen's Egg

Ingredients:
White sugar   50 g
Hen's Egg   1
Fresh ginger   some
Process and application:
Beat the egg in a bowl. Dissolve the sugar in about
half a bowl of water and heat the water until it boils. Pour
the boiled water in the egg and stir it. Add fresh ginger
juice to the water and mix it well. Take the soup once in
the morning and once in the evening each day.
Curative properties: Chronic cough.

Sesame and Crystal Sugar

Ingredients:

Uncooked sesame	15 g
Crystal sugar	10 g

Process and application:

Take an infusion of the above ingredients in hot water.

Curative properties: Persistent nocturnal cough; non-productive cough.

Peanuts

Ingredients:

Shelled peanuts	60 g

Process and application:

Cook the peanuts (by boiling or roasting). Eat the peanuts consecutively every day until the illness is fully cured.

Curative properties: Cough due to senile chronic bronchitis.

Sugarcane and Water Chestnut Extracts

Ingredients:

Sugarcane extract	3 ml
Water chestnut extract	15 ml

Process and application:

Take the extracts after mixing them with lukewarm boiled water.

Curative properties: Chronic cough.

Hen's Eggs Stewed in Vinegar

Ingredients:

Hen's eggs	2
Vinegar	50 ml

Process and application:
Beat the eggs in a bowl of water and eat them after stewing them in vinegar.

Curative properties: Dry cough with little phlegm.

Black Bone Hen

Ingredients:

Black bone hen	1
Mature vinegar	1500 g

Process and application:
Deplume and gut the hen. Carve it into pieces and cook it in mature vinegar until it is overdone. Take it in 3 or 4 separate doses.

Curative properties: Chronic cough with dyspnea.

Lotus Root Starch with Honey

Ingredients:

Lotus root starch	30 g
Honey	30 g

Process and application:
Dissolve the lotus root starch in a little lukewarm water, pour in hot boiled water and add honey after a moment. Take this infusion warm.

Curative properties: Cough.

Decoction of Carrot and Chinese-date

Ingredients:

Carrot	150 g
Chinese-dates	15

Process and application:

Decoct the above ingredients in two bowlfuls of water in a pot until one bowl of decoction is left. Take the decoction in 3 separate doses in one day, for 3 to 5 consecutive days.

Curative properties: Cough.

Lotus Root Juice and Honey

Ingredients:

Fresh lotus root	some
Honey	15 - 30 g

Process and application:

Wash the lotus root clean and extract 100 - 150 ml of its juice. Take 50 - 100 ml of the juice after adding honey at a time, 2 or 3 times a day.

Curative properties: Cough.

Crystal Sugar and Bananas

Ingredients:

Bananas	1 or 2
Crystal sugar	some

Process and application:

Put the bananas(peeled) and crystal sugar in a container. Cook them by putting the container in boiling water. Take them once or twice a day, for several consecutive days.

Curative properties: Chronic cough.

Fried Hen's Egg with Fresh Ginger

Ingredients:

Hen's egg	1
Fresh ginger	10 g

Process and application:
Beat the egg, mix it with chopped fresh ginger and fry it in oil. Take it twice a day.

Curative properties: Cough.

Honey with Hen's Egg

Ingredients:

Honey	35 g
Hen's egg	1

Process and application:
Boil the honey in 300 ml of water, beat the egg in it and continue heating it until it simmers. Take it all in one draft, in the morning or in the evening on an empty stomach.

Curative properties: Chronic cough.

Fried Hen's Egg with Chinese Chives

Ingredients:

Chinese chives	100 g
Hen's eggs	2

Process and application:
Wash the Chinese chives clean, chop it, mix it with the eggs and fry the mixture in oil. Eat this as a snack.

Curative properties: Cough, asthma, etc.

Honey with Fresh Ginger Extract

Ingredients:

Fresh ginger	50 g
Honey	30 g

Process and application:
Pound the fresh ginger and squeeze it to obtain its extract. Mix the extract with honey in a bowl and cook it by putting the bowl in boiling water for 10 minutes.

Curative properties: Cold, cough, etc.

BRONCHIAL ASTHMA

Walnut Kernel in White Spirit

Ingredients:

Walnut kernel	50 g
White spirit	500 g

Process and application:
Wash the walnut kernel clean, skin it and remove the impurities. Put it into a jar with white spirit and mix them even. Seal the jar hermetically and let the walnut kernel soak in it for 15 days. Stir the white spirit every other day. Take 15 g of the liquid at a time, 3 times a day.

Curative properties: Cough with asthma, hard and dry motions.

Glutinous Rice Gruel with Fresh Ginger and Chinese-date

Ingredients:

Fresh ginger	9 g
Chinese-dates	2

Glutinous rice   150 g

Process and application:

Chop the fresh ginger and cook it with glutinous rice and Chinese-dates until they become gruel.

Curative properties: Senile asthma.

Black Sesame Seed with Fresh Ginger, Honey and Crystal Sugar

Ingredients:

Black sesame seed	250 g
Fresh ginger	250 g
Honey	200 g
Crystal sugar	200 g

Process and application:

Extract the juice from the fresh ginger. Melt the crystal sugar by heating it. Roast the sesame seeds and leave them to cool off. Mix the sesame seeds with the fresh ginger juice and heat the mixture until it is dry. Then mix the dried mixture with honey and crystal sugar syrup and contain it in a bottle. Take an infusion of one spoonful of this in hot water, once in the morning and once in the evening.

Curative properties: Senile asthma.

Drink of Radish Seed and Apricot Kernel

Ingredients:

Radish seed	20 g
Apricot kernel	20 g

Process and application:

Roast the radish seeds and skin the apricot kernel. Put them with one and half bowls of water in a pot and decoct them until only half bowl of decoction is left. Take the drink twice a day.

Curative properties: Asthma with abundant expectoration.

Decoction of Sweet Almond, Bitter Apricot Kernel and Crystal Sugar

Ingredients:

Sweet almond	25 g
Bitter apricot kernel	25 g
Crystal sugar	50 g

Process and application:
Put the apricot kernel and a bowl of water in a pot and decoct them until half a bowl of decoction is left. Add the crystal sugar to the decoction and continue heating the decoction until the crystal sugar dissolves.

Curative properties: Senile asthma.

Hen's Eggs Stewed in Tea

Ingredients:

Green tea	15 g
Hen's eggs	2

Process and application:
Cook the above together until the eggs are done. Shell the eggs and continue cooking them until the water is dry. Eat the eggs at any time.

Curative properties: Asthma.

Chicken Soup with Tender Loofah

Ingredients:

Tender loofahs	3
Chicken	200 g
Table salt, cooking oil, gourmet	

18

powder and soy sauce   some for each

Process and application:

Cut the tender loofahs into thin slices, cook them with chicken in a deep pot for an hour and add some flavorings. Take this with bread or cooked rice in meal once a day, for 5 consecutive days as a course of treatment.

Curative properties: Bronchial asthma.

Lean Pork with Red Onion

Ingredients:

Lean pork	200 g
Red onions	4

Process and application:

Cook the above in water for eating.

Curative properties: Hemoptysis, spitting blood due to pulmonary tuberculosis.

Chinese Chives and Clam Meat

Ingredients:

Chinese chives	100 - 150 g
Clam meat	150 - 200 g

Process and application:

Cook the above in water and eat them with flavorings. This can also be taken with bread or cooked rice.

Curative properties: Debility due to pulmonary tuberculosis.

Pear Extract and Human Milk

Ingredients:

Fresh pears	4

Human milk   100 ml

Process and application:

Wash the pears clean and squeeze them to get 100 ml of extract; mix the extract with the human milk; put the mixture in a container and heat it by putting the container in water until the water boils.

Curative properties: Debility due to pulmonary tuberculosis.

Fresh Lotus Root and Sugar

Ingredients:

Fresh lotus root   1 section
Sugar   some

Process and application:

Cut the fresh lotus root into slices and eat them after dipping them in sugar.

Curative properties: Hemoptysis, spitting blood due to pulmonary tuberculosis.

Eel Stewed in Yellow Rice or Millet Wine and Vinegar

Ingredients:

Eel   500 g
Yellow rice or millet
   wine and vinegar   some for each

Process and application:

Cook the above for eating.

Curative properties: Low fever, hectic fever due to pulmonary tuberculosis.

Dumpling from Wheat Bran

Ingredients:

Wheat bran	100 g
Lean pork dust	250 g
Glutinous rice flour, green Chinese onion, table salt	some for each

Process and application:

Prepare dumplings by stuffing the mixture of the wheat bran, lean pork dust, green Chinese onion and salt into glutinous rice flour paste. Boil the dumplings in water and eat them.

Curative properties: Night sweat due to pulmonary tuberculosis.

Chinese Chives Juice with Brown Sugar

Ingredients:

Chinese chives	a handful
Brown sugar	a little

Process and application:

Extract the juice from Chinese chives and mix it with some water and brown sugar. Take 10 drops of the juice every day.

Curative properties: Cough due to pulmonary tuberculosis.

Tortoise Meat Gruel

Ingredients:

Tortoise meat	150 - 200 g
Rice	100 g

Process and application:

Cook the tortoise meat till it becomes soft. Prepare gruel with rice and the meat and season the gruel with cooking oil, table salt, green Chinese onion, gourmet powder etc. Eat it warm for breakfast or supper once every other day. This recipe remains effective even if used repeatedly for a long time.

Curative properties: Chronic cough and hemoptysis due to pulmonary tuberculosis.

Silkworm Chrysalis Powder

Ingredients:

Silkworm chrysalis   some

Process and application:

Dry the silkworm chrysalis over fire and grind them into a fine powder. Take 3 to 5 g of the powder at a time, twice a day. This recipe can be taken consecutively for a period of long time until the focus is calcified.

Curative properties: Pulmonary tuberculosis (This recipe speeds the focal calcification).

Lotus Root Juice with Honey and Human Milk

Ingredients:

Lotus root juice   500 g

Human milk   120 g

Honey   120 g

Process and application:

Mix the above ingredients evenly and steam the mixture for 15 minutes. Take 25 ml of the mixture once in the morning and once in the evening. Tea-drinking should be avoided.

Curative properties: Spitting blood due to pulmonary tuberculosis.

Hen's Egg Shell and Yolk Oil

Ingredients:

Hen's egg shells	6
Egg Yolks	6

Process and application:

Grind the egg-shells into fine powder and mix it with the yolks. Roast the mixture in an enamel ware or earthenware over charcoal fire and at the same time stir it until it becomes dark brown and a brown oil is extracted. Put the oil in a bowl for later use.

Curative properties: Infiltrative type of pulmonary tuberculosis.

STOMACH-ACHE

Old Ginger Jelly

Ingredients:

Old ginger	250 g
Brown sugar	250 g

Process and application:

Smash the old ginger to extract its juice, steam the juice till the water boils 10 times. Make jelly by dissolving brown sugar in it. Take the jelly once in the morning and once in the evening, for 4 consecutive days.

Curative properties: Epigastralgia.

Rose Infusion

Ingredients:

Dried rose petal	6 - 10 g (for one dose)

Process and application:

Put the petals in a tea-cup, pour in hot water and cover the cup, let the petals infuse for a moment. Take this infusion as a drink.

Curative properties: Gastric ulcer; duodenal ulcer.

Cabbage Gruel

Ingredients:

Cabbage	500 g
Rice	50 g

Process and application:

Wash the cabbage clean, chop it and boil it for half an hour. Remove the cabbage from the water and put in rice to cook gruel. Take the gruel twice a day.

Curative properties: Gastrospasm.

Spirit with Pericarp of Green Walnut

Ingredients:

Pericarps of unripe walnuts	100 g
Spirit	400 g

Process and application:

Wash the pericarps of green walnut clean. Soak them in a hermetically sealed bottle of spirit for 10 days. Take 5 ml of the liquid when a pain is felt.

Curative properties: Neurosal stomach-ache.

River Snail Shell

Ingredients:

Shell of a river snail	some
Brown sugar	some

Process and application:

Bake the shell of a river snail on a new tile over fire

until it is dry. Grind it into fine powder. Take an infusion of 15 g powder at a time in brown sugar water.

Curative properties: Stomach-ache; acid regurgitation.

Honey

Ingredients:

Honey   150 g

Process and application:

Warm the honey by putting the container in simmering water. Take it before meal, 3 times a day.

Curative properties: Gastric ulcer.

Hen's Egg Shell

Ingredients:

Hen's egg shell   1

Process and application:

Wash the egg-shell clean, parch it in a pot until it becomes yellow. Grind it into fine powder. Take an infusion of the powder in hot water once a day.

Curative properties: Stomach-ache; acid regurgitation.

White Pepper and Chinese-dates

Ingredients:

Chinese-dates   5
White pepper   10 pcs

Process and application:

Stone the Chinese-dates, stuff 2 pieces of white pepper into each of them and steam them. Take 2 or 3 Chinese-dates at a time, twice a day.

Curative properties: Stomach-ache.

Egg Soup with Fresh Chili Pepper Leaves

Ingredients:

Fresh chili pepper leaves	60 - 90 g
Hen's eggs	2

Process and application:

Shell the eggs and fry them in peanut oil. Put in one and half bowls of water and the fresh chili pepper leaves and cook soup with them. Season the soup with a little table salt and take the soup with bread or cooked rice in meal.

Curative properties: Stomach-ache.

Juice of Fresh Ginger, Tangerine and Potato

Ingredients:

New potato	100 g
Fresh ginger	10 g
Fresh tangerine juice	30 ml

Process and application:

Extract the juice from potato and fresh ginger and mix the juice with the fresh tangerine juice. Warm the combined juice by putting the container in hot water. Take 30 ml of the juice in 3 equal portions each day.

Curative properties: Neurosal stomach-ache; nausea; vomiting.

Steamed Crucian Carp with White Pepper Powder

Ingredients:

Crucian carp (live, of no less than 200 g)	1
White pepper powder	20 g

Process and application:

Gut the crucian carp, stuff it with white pepper powder and steam it until it is done. The curative effect will be achieved after taking this several times.

Curative properties: Various chronic stomach-ache.

Ham Seasoned with Salt and Prickly-ash Peel

Ingredients:

Ham of lean meat	25 g
Prickly-ash peel, table salt, green Chinese onion, ginger	some for each

Process and application:

Cut the ham into slices. Put the slices, green Chinese onion and ginger in water and steam them until the meat becomes very soft. Roast the prickly-ash peel in another pot until it becomes brown. Put in some salt and continue heating the mixture of salt and prickly-ash peel for a moment and put this mixture in a plate for later use. Eat the ham after dipping it in the prickly-ash peel and salt, at a draft or in doses.

Curative properties: Stomach-ache.

Milk with Chinese Chives and Fresh Ginger

Ingredients:

Chinese chives	250 g
Fresh ginger	25 g
Milk	250 g (or 2 spoonfuls of milk powder)

Process and application:

Wash the Chinese chives and fresh ginger clean and chop them. Wrap them in gauze to squeeze the juice out.

Mix the juice with milk in a pot and heat the milk until it boils. Drink the milk hot.

Curative properties: Chronic gastritis; gastric ulcer; nausea; vomiting.

Dried Ginger and Pepper Powder

Ingredients:

Dried ginger	10 g
Pepper	10 pcs

Process and application:

Grind the above ingredients into powder and take it after infusing it in hot water. Take all the powder in 2 doses in one day.

Curative properties: Stomach-ache.

Hen's Egg Fried in Sesame Oil with Fresh Ginger

Ingredients:

Hen's egg	1
Fresh ginger	30 g

Process and application:

Shell the egg, mix it with fresh ginger dust and fry it in sesame oil. Take it all in 3 doses in one day. Take this for 3 to 5 consecutive days.

Curative properties: Stomach-ache.

Chinese-date Syrup with Fresh Ginger

Ingredients:

Fresh ginger	1500 g
Chinese-date	1500 g
Brown sugar	2000 g

Rape-seed oil   100 g

Process and application:

Wash the fresh ginger and Chinese-date clean and cut the fresh ginger into slices. Put some rapeseed oil in an iron pot and heat the oil over fire. When the oil is hot, fry the fresh ginger slices in it until the oil gets dry. Put in Chinese-date and 5000 ml of water and cook them until the Chinese-date becomes very soft. Strain the dregs from the liquid and mix the brown sugar in the decoction. Heat the mixture over soft fire until it becomes syrup. Take 1 or 2 spoonfuls of the syrup (infused in hot water) each time, twice a day.

Curative properties: Gastric ulcer; duodenal ulcer.

Potato Gruel

Ingredients:

Potato (unpeeled)   250 g

Honey   a little

Process and application:

Cut the potato into cubes and boil them in water. Mix honey in the gruel and eat it on an empty stomach in the early morning, for half a month as a course of treatment.

Curative properties: Vague pain in gastric cavity.

Cactus Powder

Ingredients:

Fresh cactus   any amount

Process and application:

Remove the thorns of the fresh cactus and wash it clean. Slice it and dry it in sun. When dry, grind it into fine powder and keep the powder in a bottle or in capsules. Take an infusion of 1 g powder in lukewarm boiled water each time on an empty stomach, twice a day.

Curative properties: Gastric ulcer; duodenal ulcer; burning pain in gastric cavity, hematochezia due to chronic or acute gastritis.

Milk with Peanuts and Honey

Ingredients:

Shelled peanuts	50 g
Fresh milk	250 ml
White honey (refined)	30 ml

Process and application:

Wash the peanuts clean, leave them soak in clear water for 30 minutes, fish them out and pound them. Boil the milk, put in the pounded peanuts and stew the milk over soft fire for a while. Remove it from the fire, leave it to cool off and mix it with some honey. Take the milk before sleep every night. This recipe can be taken for a period of time.

Curative properties: Chronic ulcer of digestive tract; loss of appetite; constipation.

Chinese Yam Mash with Honey and Sugar

Ingredients:

Honey	50 g
White sugar	50 g
Fresh Chinese yam	250 g

Process and application:

Peel the Chinese yam, wash it clean, slice it and boil it with sugar in a little water until the Chinese yam becomes very soft. Remove it from fire, leave it to cool off, mash it, add some honey and steam it for 15 minutes, and thus a dosage for one day is prepared. Take it hot 3 times a day on an empty stomach, for one week as a course of treatment.

Curative properties: Gastric ulcer, duodenal ulcer with complication of hard and dry motions or hemorrhage of digestive tract.

VOMITING

Milk with Chinese Chives and Fresh Ginger Juice

Ingredients:

Milk	250 ml
Chinese chives juice	60 ml
Fresh ginger juice	15 ml

Process and application:
Boil the milk, remove it from fire and leave it cool until it becomes lukewarm. Add the Chinese chives juice and fresh ginger juice to it. Drink the mixture at any time.

Curative properties: Hiccup; regurgitation; vomiting right after eating.

Fresh Ginger Juice and Honey

Ingredients:

Fresh ginger juice	1 spoonful
Honey	2 spoonfuls

Process and application:
Add 3 spoonfuls of boiled water to the above ingredients and steam the mixture. Take it all at a time.

Curative properties: Persistent vomiting.

Sugarcane Juice and Honey

Ingredients:

Sugarcane juice	50 ml
Honey	30 g

Process and application:

Mix the above ingredients and take the mixture twice a day, once in the morning and once in the evening.

Curative properties: Regurgitation and vomiting; bitter taste; anorexia.

White Hyaciath Bean Gruel

Ingredients:

Roasted white hyaciath bean	60 g (or fresh white hyaciath bean 120 g)
Rice	100 g

Process and application:

Prepare gruel with the above ingredients. Eat the gruel in the morning and evening.

Curative properties: Loss of appetite with hiccup; diarrhea and dysentery in summer and autumn.

Tangerine Peel Gruel

Ingredients:

Tangerine peel	15 g
Rice	100 g
White sugar	some

Process and application:

This diet is prepared in 2 alternative ways: (1.) Wash the tangerine peel clean, dry it over heat, grind it into fine powder. Add the powder to cooked gruel and keep the gruel boiling for a moment. Eat the gruel after adding sugar to it. (2.) Boil the washed tangerine peel for about 20 minutes, strain the decoction, cook washed rice in the decoction until it becomes gruel. Eat the gruel after adding sugar. This recipe can be taken regularly.

Curative properties: Anorexia; vomiting. This recipe can also be used as an antidote to food poisoning caused by fish or crabs.

Mango

Ingredients:
Mangoes   a few
Process and application:
Wash the mangoes clean, pack them in a plastic bag with its opening tied up so as to keep them fresh.
Curative properties: Vomiting.

Radish and Honey

Ingredients:
Radish   1
Honey   50 g
Process and application:
Wash the radish clean, chop and pulp it. Eat it in 2 portions after mixing it with honey.
Curative properties: Regurgitation and vomiting.

Sugarcane and Fresh Ginger Juice

Ingredients:
Sugarcane juice   half a cup
Fresh ginger juice   1 spoonful
Process and application:
Peel the sugarcane, smash it and squeeze its juice out. Squeeze the juice of fresh ginger out and combine the juices together. Drink the combined juice warm.

Curative properties: Regurgitation and vomiting or

persistent retching due to early stage of carcinoma of stomach, reaction of pregnancy or chronic gastropathy.

Milk Stewed with Chinese Chives Juice and Fresh Ginger Juice

Ingredients:

Fresh Chinese chives juice	2 spoonfuls
Fresh ginger juice	1 spoonful
Fresh milk	250 ml

Process and application:

Mix the above ingredients, put them in a container and heat the mixture by putting the container in hot water until it is done. Take the mixture before meal.

Curative properties: Dysphagia and regurgitation; vomiting right after eating.

White Radish Preserved in Honey

Ingredients:

White radish	500 g
Honey	150 g

Process and application:

Wash the white radish clean, cut it into cubes, boil the cubes in water, strain off the liquid and dry them in sun for half a day. Put the cubes with honey in an aluminum pan, stew them over soft fire until the honey boils. Stir the mixture, leave it cool and keep it in a bottle for later use. Take 2 spoonfuls of the mixture each time, twice a day, once in the morning and once in the evening.

Curative properties: Nausea and vomiting.

Mutton and Garlic

Ingredients:

Mutton and garlic   some for each

Process and application:

Remove the fat from the mutton and cook it until it is done. Eat it with flavoring of garlic.

Curative properties: Regurgitation; vomiting.

MALDIGESTION

Rice Gruel with Tea

Ingredients:

Tea   6 g

Rice   100 g

Process and application:

Let the tea infuse in hot water for 6 minutes, strain the tea, cook the washed rice in the tea until it becomes gruel. Eat the gruel once a day.

Curative properties: Maldigestion.

Red Bayberry Infused in Spirit

Ingredients:

Red bayberry and spirit   some for each

Process and application:

Wash the red bayberry clean, dry it and leave it soak in spirit for 3 months in a hermetically sealed container. Take the spirit with bread or cooked rice.

Curative properties: Maldigestion.

Fried Pork and Carrot

Ingredients:

Carrot	250 g
Pork	100 g
Cooking oil	25 g
Green Chinese onion	some
Fresh ginger	some
Coriander	some
Table salt	some
Soy sauce	some
Vinegar	some
Gourmet powder	some
Sesame oil	some

Process and application:

Wash the carrot clean and shred it. Shred the pork. Heat some cooking oil in a pan and when the oil is hot, put in the green Chinese onion shred, fresh ginger dust and the pork to stir-fry. Then add shredded carrot, vinegar, soy sauce and salt and continue to fry them. When the pork is done, season it with gourmet powder, coriander and sesame oil.

Curative properties: Malnutrition due to maldigestion.

Fig Infusion

Ingredients:

Dried figs	2
White sugar	some

Process and application:

Smash the figs and roast them until they become half brown. Take an infusion of the figs in hot water with sugar as a drink.

Curative properties: Maldigestion.

White Radish Pie

Ingredients:

White radish	150 g
Wheat flour	150 g
Lean pork	60 g
Green Chinese onion, fresh ginger,	
soya-bean oil, table salt	some for each

Process and application:

Shred the washed white radish, fry it in soya-bean oil until it is half done. Prepare the stuffing by mixing it with mashed pork. Prepare pastry by mixing water and flour, fill the pastry with the stuffing to make meat pies and bake them in a pan.

Curative properties: Anorexia; maldigestion; epigastric distension after meal.

Gruel with Pineapple and Honey

Ingredients:

Pineapple flesh	100 g
Honey	50 g
Rice	80 g

Process and application:

Cook the rice in water, add pineapple and honey and keep the gruel boiling for 5 - 10 minutes. Eat the gruel warm once a day.

Curative properties: Anorexia; maldigestion.

CONSTIPATION

Honey Tea

Ingredients:

Tea   3 g
Honey   2 ml

Process and application:

Infuse the above ingredients in hot water. Drink one cup of the infusion after meal.

Curative properties: Constipation.

Chinese Cabbage Juice

Ingredients:

Chinese cabbage   some

Process and application:

Extract the juice of Chinese cabbage and boil it. Take the juice as a drink.

Curative properties: Hard and dry motions, dysporia.

Honeysuckle Flower Decoction with Honey

Ingredients:

Honeysuckle flower   30 g
Honey   20 g

Process and application:

Put the honeysuckle flower and 2 bowls of water in a pot and boil it until one bowl of decoction is left. Strain the decoction and add the honey to it. Take the decoction twice a day, once in the morning and once in the evening.

Curative properties: Senile constipation.

Chinese Chives Juice and White Spirit

Ingredients:

Chinese chives juice	1 cup
White spirit	half a cup
Boiled water	half a cup

Process and application:

Mix the above ingredients for drinking.

Curative properties: Habitual constipation.

Lard in White Spirit

Ingredients:

Lard (a lump in size of half an egg, cut into pieces)	some
White spirit	250 g

Process and application:

Heat the white spirit until it simmers, put in the lard and keep the white spirit boiling for a moment. Divide the whole decoction into 2 doses. Take it warm before meal. If the symptom remains, take another dose.

Curative properties: Constipation; anuresis.

Rice Gruel with Kernels

Ingredients:

Sesame	10 g
Shelled pine nut	10 g
Shelled walnut	10 g
Shelled and roasted peach kernel	10 g
Sweet almond	10 g
Rice	200 g

Process and application:

Mix the above kernels and grind them into powder, cook gruel with the powder and rice and when the gruel is done, add some sugar. Eat the gruel in the morning and evening.

Curative properties: Constipation.

Taro Gruel

Ingredients:

Rice	50 g
Taro	250 g

Process and application:

Peel the taro, cut it into cubes and cook gruel with them and rice. Eat the gruel after seasoning it with salt and cooking oil.

Curative properties: Hard and dry motions.

Spinach and Rice Gruel

Ingredients:

Fresh spinach	100 g
Rice	100 g

Process and application:

Wash the spinach clean, soak it in hot water until it is half done, fish it out and cut it into pieces. Cook gruel with rice and, when done, put in the spinach, stir the gruel and continue heating the gruel till it boils. Take the gruel twice a day.

Curative properties: Constipation.

Pine Nut Kernel Gruel

Ingredients:

Pine nut kernel	15 g

Rice   30 g
Process and application:
Cook rice in water until it becomes gruel. Put in pestled pine nut kernels and keep the gruel boiling for a while. Take the gruel on an empty stomach.
Curative properties: Senile constipation.

Carrot with Honey

Ingredients:
Carrot and honey   some for each
Process and application:
Boil the carrot until it is done and eat it with honey. Take 250 to 500 g of it each time, twice a day.
Curative properties: Constipation.

Banana and Black Sesame Seed

Ingredients:
Banana   500 g
Black sesame seed   25 g
Process and application:
Roast the black sesame seeds until they are half done. Eat the banana after dusting it with sesame seeds. Take all the ingredients in 3 portions in the same day.
Curative properties: Constipation; hypertension.

Milk, Honey and Green Chinese Onion Juice

Ingredients:
Milk   250 ml
Honey   100 ml
Green Chinese onion juice   a little
Process and application:

Take the above ingredients after boiling them every morning.

Curative properties: Habitual constipation.

Steamed Banana and Crystal Sugar

Ingredients:

Bananas	2
Crystal sugar	some

Process and application:

Peel the bananas and steam them with crystal sugar until they become soft. Take them twice a day, for several consecutive days.

Curative properties: This recipe is efficacious for constipation of weak patients.

Mulberry Syrup

Ingredients:

Fresh mulberry	1000 g
Honey	300 g

Process and application:

Decoct the mulberry, strain off the liquid, add the same amount of water to the mulberry and decoct it again. Combine the 2 decoctions together and heat the combined decoction (about 1000 ml) over slow fire until it becomes thick and sticky. Add honey and heat it until it boils. Remove it from fire, leave it cool and preserve it in a bottle. Take 20 ml of this syrup with some warm water at a time, 2 or 3 times a day.

Curative properties: Constipation due to caducity.

Mash of Black Sesame Seed, Apricot Kernel and Rice

Ingredients:

Black sesame seed	150 g
Apricot kernel	100 g
Rice	150 g

Process and application:
Soak the above in water, mash them and cook them together. Eat the mash after adding some sugar to it.

Curative properties: Constipation.

Wax-gourd Custard

Ingredients:

Wax-gourd	500 g
Pork	200 g
Shelled fresh shrimps	20 g

Process and application:
Boil the pork (sliced) for an hour, put in the slices of wax-gourd (peeled), shelled fresh shrimps and salt and continue cooking them for 20 minutes until the soup becomes thick and smells good. Add gourmet powder to it. Eat the custard with bread or cooked rice in meal. It is helpful to take this recipe often.

Curative properties: Habitual constipation.

Sugarcane Juice

Ingredients:

Sugarcane	1000 g
White sugar	50 g

Process and application:
Peel the sugarcane, chop it, squeeze its juice out and

add some sugar to the juice. Drink all the juice in one dose. This recipe can be taken often.

Curative properties: Anorexia for children; alcoholic intoxication; constipation etc.

DIARRHEA (ACUTE AND CHRONIC ENTERITIS, INTESTINAL TUBERCULOSIS, INTESTINAL DYSFUNCTION, ETC.)

Strong Tea and Vinegar

Ingredients:

Strong tea	1 cup
Vinegar	a little

Process and application:

Add a little vinegar to a cup of strong tea for drinking.

Curative properties: Thirst; diarrhea.

Dried Ginger and Tea

Ingredients:

Green tea	6 g
Dried ginger dust	3 g

Process and application:

Let the green tea and dried ginger dust infuse in boiled water for 10 minutes. Take it as a drink. Stop drinking it as soon as diarrhea is arrested. It is inadvisable to use this recipe often.

Curative properties: Enteritis; bacillary dysentery.

Pomegranate Rind Tea

Ingredients:

Pomegranate rind   5 g
Process and application:
Grind the pomegranate rind into powder and boil it in water. Take it as a drink.
Curative properties: Protracted dysentery.

Hen's Egg with Boiled White Spirit

Ingredients:
White spirit   some
Hen's eggs   2
Process and application:
Boil the white spirit and pour it on shelled eggs.
Curative properties: Acute diarrhea.

"One-clove Garlic*" Boiled in White Spirit

Ingredients:
One-clove garlic   1
White spirit   some
Process and application:
Cook the garlic with brown sugar in white spirit.
Curative properties: Watery diarrhea.

Lotus Seed Soaked in White Spirit

Ingredients:
Lotus seed   50 g
White spirit   500 ml
Process and application:
Skin the lotus seeds and remove the kernels. Wash

---

* One-clove garlic — a var. of garlic (*Bulbus Allii*), bulb of which consists of only one clove.

them clean and put them in a jar full of white spirit. Seal the jar hermetically and leave them infuse in it for 15 days, during which they are stirred every other day. Take 15 - 20 ml of the liquid at a time, twice a day.

Curative properties: Diarrhea.

Chinese Yam and Rice Gruel

Ingredients:

Fresh Chinese yam	120 g
Rice	100 g

Process and application:

Cook gruel with the above ingredients. Eat the gruel in the morning and evening.

Curative properties: Chronic enteritis.

Ginseng and Rice Gruel

Ingredients:

Ginseng	5 g (or pilose asiabell root 15 g)
Rice	100 g

Process and application:

Cook gruel with the above ingredients and add a little crystal sugar. Eat the gruel in the morning and evening.

Curative properties: Chronic gastroenteritis.

Chinese-date and Glutinous Rice Gruel

Ingredients:

Chinese-date	15 g
Glutinous rice	60 g

Process and application:

After soaking the Chinese-date in water for one hour, cook it and rice in water to prepare gruel. Eat the gruel in the morning and evening.

Curative properties: Chronic gastroenteritis.

Chinese Yam and Mutton Gruel

Ingredients:

Mutton	250 g
Fresh Chinese yam	500 g
Glutinous rice	some

Process and application:

Cook the mutton and Chinese yam until they become soft. Put in rice and some water to cook them until they become gruel.

Curative properties: Diarrhea.

Lichee Gruel

Ingredients:

Dried lichee flesh	50 g
Chinese yam	10 g
Lotus seed	10 g
Rice	some

Process and application:

Pestle the lichee flesh, Chinese yam and lotus seeds, cook them in water until they become very soft. Then add washed rice and continue cooking them until they become thin gruel. Eat the gruel in the evening.

Curative properties: Diarrhea before dawn.

Roasted Rice Gruel

Ingredients:

Rice	100 g

Process and application:

Roast the rice until it becomes brown, cook it in water until it becomes gruel. Eat the gruel at any time.

Curative properties: Anorexia; watery diarrhea.

Chinese Yam Gruel with Egg Yolk

Ingredients:

Chinese yam	50 g
Hen's egg yolks	2

Process and application:

Grind the Chinese yam and sift the powder through a sieve. Cook the powder in some water for a while, then put in the yolks. Take this 3 time a day on an empty stomach.

Curative properties: Protracted diarrhea.

Parched Wheat Flour and Glutinous Rice with Chinese-date Powder

Ingredients:

Wheat flour, glutinous rice and Chinese-date
equal amount for each

Process and application:

Parch the wheat flour and glutinous rice until they become yellow. Stone the Chinese-date, bake it dry and grind all the above ingredients into fine powder. Take an infusion of 25 - 50 g of the powder in hot water each time.

Curative properties: Diarrhea before dawn.

Parched Wheat Flour and Rice Flour

Ingredients:

Rice flour	250 g
Wheat flour	250 g

Process and application:
Parch the above flours in an iron pot. Leave the flour to cool off. Take an infusion of the flour in hot water after adding some sugar to it, at any time.

Curative properties: Chronic diarrhea.

Lotus-seed Kernel Patty

Ingredients:

Lotus-seed kernels	some
Glutinous rice (or ordinary rice)	500 g

Process and application:
Boil the lotus-seed kernels in water until they become soft, wrap them in gauze and press them into mash. Mix the mash with washed glutinous rice and steam it. After it cools off, press the mash into patties, carve them up and dust them with sugar.

Curative properties: Pollakicoprosis; failing appetite; ochriasis.

Duck-egg Boiled in Vinegar

Ingredients:

Duck-eggs	1 or 2
Vinegar	250 g

Process and application:
Boil the duck-eggs in vinegar. Eat the eggs with the vinegar.

Curative properties: Chronic gastroenteritis.

Parched Rice Powder with Fresh Ginger Soup

Ingredients:

Rice and fresh ginger	some for each

Process and application:
Roast the rice in an iron pot until it becomes dark. Grind it into fine powder. Take an infusion of 5 g powder before meal in fresh ginger soup.

Curative properties: Chronic gastroenteritis.

Cooked Yellow Hen and Lotus-seed Kernel

Ingredients:

Yellow hen	1
Lotus-seed kernel	150 g

Process and application:
Deplume and gut the yellow hen, wash it clean and cook it along with lotus-seed kernels until they become very soft.

Curative properties: Diarrhea.

Pickled Leaf of Chinese Toon

Ingredients:

Fresh leaf of Chinese toon	some

Process and application:
Wash the leaf of Chinese toon clean and leave it to dry. Pickle it in table salt of a tenth of the leaf's weight for several days, dry it in sun and preserve it for use.

Curative properties: Chronic diarrhea.

Hen's Egg with Sugar in White Spirit

Ingredients:

Hen's egg	1
White sugar	10 g
White spirit	100 ml

Process and application:

Beat the egg in a bowl, put in white sugar, pour in the white spirit and stir it. Light the white spirit, stir the white spirit while it is burning until all the white spirit is burnt out and the egg rises like a flower. Eat the egg after it cools down.

Curative properties: Diarrhea.

Hen's Eggs Boiled in Rice Vinegar

Ingredients:

Hen's eggs	3
Fresh ginger	15 g
Rice vinegar	15 ml

Process and application:

Beat the egg. Cut the fresh ginger into small pieces. Mix the egg with fresh ginger, some table salt and green Chinese onion and fry them in cooking oil until they become a patty. Boil the fried egg in rice vinegar and eat it as a snack.

Curative properties: Diarrhea.

DYSENTERY

Hawthorn Fruit Syrup in White Spirit

Ingredients:

Hawthorn fruit	60 g
Brown sugar	60 g
White spirit	30 ml

Process and application:

Roast the hawthorn fruit over soft fire until it turns light brown, remove it from fire, mix it with white spirit and boil the mixture in 200 ml of water for 15 minutes. Strain the liquid and put in brown sugar. Take the liquid hot in one draft, once a day.

Curative properties: Acute bacillary dysentery

Purslane Gruel

Ingredients:

Purslane	2 full handfuls
Rice	100 g
White sugar	some

Process and application:
Wash the purslane clean, cut it into pieces. Wash the rice clean and cook it in water to prepare gruel. As the gruel turns thick, put in the purslane and heat the gruel until it boils. Eat the gruel warm after adding some sugar to it, twice a day.

Curative properties: Dysentery with bloody stool.

Dried Snail Meat Soup

Ingredients:

Dried snail meat	some

Process and application:
Parch the dried snail meat until it becomes dark brown and decoct it in water. Take 15 g of the decoction at a time, 3 times a day.

Curative properties: Dysentery.

Fig Decoction and Sugar

Ingredients:

Figs	several
White sugar	a little

Process and application:
Pulp the figs, cook them with sugar in clear water in

an earthenware pot. Take all the decoction with the flesh of figs.

Curative properties: Dysentery.

Purple-skin Garlic and Glutinous Rice Gruel

Ingredients:

Purple-skin garlic (skinned)	30 g
Glutinous rice	100 g

Process and application:

Boil the purple-skin garlic in water and fish it out. Cook the glutinous rice in the decoction until it becomes thin gruel. Put the garlic back in the pot and continue cooking the gruel for a moment. Take the gruel once in the morning and once in the evening.

Curative properties: Acute and chronic dysentery in old age.

Garlic Infusion

Ingredients:

Garlic	2 bulbs
White sugar and brown sugar	a little for each

Process and application:

Pulp the garlic, leave it infuse in hot water for half a day. Strain off the infusion. Take the infusion after adding white sugar and brown sugar to it.

Curative properties: Dysentery.

Green Tea and Vinegar

Ingredients:

Green tea	100 g

Vinegar	10 ml

Process and application:

Boil the green tea in water until the infusion is condensed to 300 ml. Take 100 ml of the hot infusion with 10 ml of vinegar at a time, 3 times a day. The insomniac should avoid taking this recipe at night.

Curative properties: Dysentery.

Grape and Fresh Ginger Juice

Ingredients:

Grape and fresh ginger	some for each

Process and application:

Wash the grapes and fresh ginger clean, chop them, then wrap them in gauze and squeeze their juices out separately. Make a cup of green tea, add 50 ml of the grape juice, 50 ml of fresh ginger juice and some honey to it. Take it hot in one draft.

Curative properties: Bacillary dysentery.

Steamed Hen's Egg with Fresh Ginger

Ingredients:

Fresh ginger	9 g
Hen's egg	1

Process and application:

Pound the fresh ginger, beat the egg, mix them and steam them until they are done. Take them twice a day on an empty stomach.

Curative properties: Dysentery.

Brown Sugar and Hen's Egg

Ingredients:

| Brown sugar | 120 g |
| Hen's egg | 1 |

Process and application:

Boil 300 ml of water, dissolve the brown sugar in it, beat the egg in it and continue boiling the water until the egg is done. Take the egg in a draft, twice a day, for 3 consecutive days as a course of treatment.

Curative properties: Dysentery with blood and mucus.

"One-clove Garlic" and Hen's Egg

Ingredients:

| One-clove garlic* | 2 bulbs |
| Hen's egg | 1 |

Process and application:

Put the one-clove garlic in a pot over fire, beat the egg over the garlic, cover the pot tightly and heat it until the garlic is cooked. Take it on an empty stomach and keep on using it till the disease is cured.

Curative properties: Dysentery.

Grape Juice and Brown Sugar

Ingredients:

| Grape | 250 g |
| Brown sugar | some |

Process and application:

Wash the grapes clean, squeeze the juice out, mix the juice with brown sugar and drink the mixture at a draft. Take the juice several times until the disease is cured.

Curative properties: Dysentery with bloody stool.

---

* One-clove garlic — a var. of garlic(*Bulbus Allii*), bulb of which consists of only one clove.

Bamboo Shoot and Rice Gruel

Ingredients:

Fresh bamboo shoot	50 g
Rice	100 g
Cooking oil, table salt, shredded fresh ginger, gourmet powder	some for each

Process and application:

Cook gruel with above ingredients. Eat the gruel warm as breakfast or supper, once a day, for 10 consecutive days as a course of treatment.

Curative properties: Chronic and persistent dysentery.

Leaf of Chinese Toon Gruel

Ingredients:

Leaf of Chinese toon	80 g
Rice	100 g
Sesame oil and table salt	some for each

Process and application:

Prepare rice gruel, put in the leaf of Chinese toon (pieces), salt, sesame oil and continue cooking the gruel for a moment. Take the gruel warm once a day, for 7 consecutive days as a course of treatment.

Curative properties: Dysentery; urinary tract infection etc.

HEPATITIS

Infusion of Black Tea with Sugar

Ingredients:

Black tea	3 g
Glucose	18 g

White sugar   60 g

Process and application:

Infuse the above ingredients in hot boiled water until the infusion turns blood-red, put in more water to get 500 ml of infusion. Take all the infusion warm before noon, for 7 consecutive days as a course of treatment. Generally 2 courses are necessary. The above dosage is for children, for adult the dosage should be doubled.

Curative properties: Acute hepatitis.

Green Tea Pill

Ingredients:

Green tea   any amount

Process and application:

Grind the green tea into powder, mix it with honey and roll the mixture into 3-g pills. Take one pill at a time, 3 or 4 times a day. Take the pills consecutively for 2 or 3 weeks.

Curative properties: Acute infectious hepatitis.

Pig Liver and Rice Gruel

Ingredients:

Pig liver   100 g

Rice   100 g

Green Chinese onion, fresh ginger, table salt, sesame oil, soy sauce   some for each

Process and application:

Wash the pig liver, green Chinese onion and fresh ginger clean and cut them into small pieces separately. Soak pig liver and fresh ginger in soy sauce. Cook gruel with washed rice and when the gruel is done, put in the pig liver, continue heating the gruel for a moment and put in sesame oil and green Chinese onion. This recipe can be often taken.

Curative properties: Acute hepatitis; chronic hepatitis; night blindness; anemia.

Ham and Red Phaseolus Bean Soup

Ingredients:

Ham	250 g
Red phaseolus bean	120 g

Process and application:
Boil the above till the broth becomes thick. Take a bowl of the broth and eat all the meat and red phaseolus bean, once a day, for 7 weeks as a course of treatment.

Curative properties: Ascites due to cirrhosis of liver.

Decoction of Chinese-date, Peanut and Brown Sugar

Ingredients:

Chinese-date	50 g
Peanut	50 g
Brown sugar	50 g

Process and application:
Decoct the above ingredients in water and take the decoction once a day, for 30 days as a course of treatment.

Curative properties: Chronic hepatitis; cirrhosis of liver.

Tomato and Beef Broth

Ingredients:

Fresh tomato	450 g
Beef	100 g

Process and application:
Wash the tomato clean and cut it into cubes. Cut the beef into slices. Cook them with a little cooking oil, table salt and sugar in water. Take the broth with bread or cooked rice.

Curative properties: Chronic hepatitis.

Fried Silkworm Chrysalises

Ingredients:
Silkworm chrysalises, cooking oil, table salt, green Chinese onion, fresh ginger and garlic some for each
Process and application:
Wash the silkworm chrysalises clean and drain off the water. Heat oil in a pot and when the oil is hot, put in silkworm chrysalises and stir-fry them. Strain off most of the oil, leaving a little oil in the pot to fry the green Chinese onion, fresh ginger, garlic, table salt, etc.

Curative properties: Hepatitis; cirrhosis of liver.

Pear Soaked in Vinegar

Ingredients:
Vinegar and pear   any amount for each
Process and application:
Peel the pear and let it soak in vinegar for 3 days. This recipe produces good effect if used often.

Curative properties: Chronic hepatitis.

Mung Bean and Chinese-date Gruel

Ingredients:
Mung bean   100 g
Chinese-date   50 g

White sugar   100 g

Process and application:
Boil the mung bean and Chinese-date together until they become very soft and put in sugar.

Curative properties: Chronic hepatitis.

Bone from the Carcass of a Pig in Sweet and Sour Sauce

Ingredients:

Bone from the carcass of a pig (fresh)	500 g
Mature rice vinegar	1000 g
Brown sugar	200 g
White sugar	200 g

Process and application:
Smash and wash the bone from the carcass of a pig, cook it with sugar in mature rice vinegar(do not add water) until the mature rice vinegar boils. Move it over to slow fire and heat it for 20 minutes. Strain off the broth and preserve it after cooling. Keep the broth in a cold place. Take the broth half an hour before meal, 3 times daily. The dosage for adult is 30 - 40 ml each time, for children younger than 10, 15 - 20 ml. A course lasts 30 days and usually 2 or 3 courses are necessary.

Curative properties: Chronic persisting hepatitis. The patient of acute hepatitis with complication of high fever should not use this diet.

ICTERUS (ACUTE INFECTIOUS HEPATITIS, DISEASES OF BILIARY TRACT, HEMOLYTIC JAUNDICE, ETC)

Rice Gruel with Purple Aubergine

Ingredients:

| Purple aubergine | 1000 g |
| Rice | 150 g |

Process and application:

Wash the purple aubergine clean and cut it into pieces, prepare gruel with it and rice. Take the gruel for several consecutive days.

Curative properties: Icterohepatitis.

Drink of Chaff, Hen's Eggs and Honey

Ingredients:

Chaff	100 g
Hen's eggs	2
Honey	50 g

Process and application:

Decoct the chaff in two bowls of water until one bowl of decoction is left, strain off the decoction, beat the eggs in the decoction and mix honey with it, continue boiling the decoction until the eggs are done. Take this once a day.

Curative properties: Acute icterohepatitis.

Decoction of Soy Bean and Peking Cabbage

Ingredients:

| Soy bean | 60 g |
| Peking cabbage | 45 g |

Process and application:

Decoct the above ingredients and take the decoction.

Curative properties: Infectious icterohepatitis.

Hen's Egg with White Pepper

Ingredients:

| Fresh hen's egg | 1 |
| White pepper | 7 pcs |

Process and application:

Cut a hole in the egg, insert the white pepper through the hole, seal the egg with paste, wrap the egg with a piece of moist paper and steam the egg. Eat the egg after shelling it. The dosage for adult is 2 eggs a day; for children, 1 egg a day; 10 days make up a course of treatment. Leave an interval of 3 days between two courses.

Curative properties: Icterohepatitis.

Celery Soup with Chinese-date

Ingredients:

| Celery | 200 - 400 g |
| Chinese-date | 50 - 100 g |

Process and application:

Cook soup with the above ingredients and take the soup in separate doses.

Curative properties: Acute icterohepatitis.

Leaf Lard

Ingredients:

| Leaf lard | 90 g |

Process and application:

Melt the leaf lard and leave it to cool off. Take it all in one draft.

Curative properties: Icterohepatitis, hepatospleno-megaly.

River Snail Soup

Ingredients:

| River snail | 10 - 20 |
| Yellow rice or millet wine | half a cup |

Process and application:

Wash the river snail in clean water, remove the shells, mix the flesh with yellow rice or millet wine and stew them in water over slow fire. Take the soup once a day.

Curative properties: Icterus.

EDEMA, ASCITES (MAINLY DUE TO BILHARZIAL INFECTION, NEPHRITIS AND ASCITES DUE TO CIRRHOSIS)

Drink of Garlic and Watermelon

Ingredients:

| Garlic | 100 - 150 g |
| Watermelon | 1 |

Process and application:

Wash the watermelon clean, cut a triangular hole in it, put in the garlic(skinned) and cover the hole with the piece of rind that has just been cut down. Put the watermelon in a plate and steam it. Take the watermelon flesh hot 3 times a day.

Curative properties: Ascites due to cirrhosis; edema due to acute nephritis and chronic nephritis.

Decoction of Crucian Carp and Red Phaseolus Bean

Ingredients:

| Crucian carp (or carp) | 1 (weight about 500 g.) |
| Red phaseolus bean | 500 g |

Process and application:

Descale the crucian carp and gut it, boil it with red phaseolus bean in water until they are very soft. Strain the decoction and take the decoction hot without any seasoning for consecutive days.

Curative properties: Ascites due to portal hypertension.

Soup of Mung Bean and Garlic

Ingredients:

Mung bean	400 g
Garlic (skinned)	2 bulbs
White sugar	a little

Process and application:

Let the mung bean soak in water for 4 hours, put in the garlic and heat the water until the water boils. Move them to slow fire, continue heating them until the mung bean is very soft and season the soup with white sugar. Take the soup in 3 separate doses every day, for 7 consecutive days as a course of treatment. Stop taking this soup if the patient is not on the mend after 2 courses.

Curative properties: Ascites due to late stage of schistosomiasis.

Hen Stewed in White Spirit

Ingredients:

Hen	1
White spirit	some

Process and application:

Deplume and gut the hen and stew it in white spirit until it is done.

Curative properties: Edema of lower extremity.

Gruel of Corn(maize), White Hyaciath Bean and Chinese-date

Ingredients:

Corn	50 g
White hyaciath bean	25 g
Chinese-date	50 g

Process and application:
Prepare gruel with the above ingredients and take the gruel once a day.

Curative properties: Edema due to malnutrition.

Rice Gruel with Duck Meat

Ingredients:

Duck meat	some
Rice	some

Process and application:
Prepare gruel with the above ingredients and eat the gruel after seasoning it with salt, twice a day.

Curative properties: Edema.

Soup of Wax-gourd Peel and Broad Bean

Ingredients:

Wax-gourd peel	60 g
Broad bean	60 g

Process and application:
Put the above ingredients and 3 bowls of clear water in a pot and decoct them until 1 bowl of decoction is left. Strain off the soup and take it 3 or 4 times a day. It is prohibited for the patients who are allergic to the broad bean.

Curative properties: Edema.

Sheep Milk with White Sugar

Ingredients:

Sheep milk	500 ml
White sugar	some

Process and application:

Boil the sheep milk and add some white sugar. Take it once every morning.

Curative properties: Edema due to chronic nephritis.

Crucian Carp Cooked with Wax-gourd Peel

Ingredients:

Crucian carp	1
Wax-gourd peel	100 g

Process and application:

Gut the crucian carp and cook it with wax-gourd peel until it is very soft. Take it twice a day.

Curative properties: Ascites.

Steamed Wax-gourd

Ingredients:

Wax-gourd	50 g

Process and application:

Wash the wax-gourd clean and cut it(unskinned) into pieces, put the pieces in a bowl and steam them until they are done. Take them with cooked rice 3 times a day without seasoning of table salt.

Curative properties: Edema due to malnutrition.

Chinese-date, Garlic and Peanuts

Ingredients:

Chinese-date	15 pcs
Peanut kernels	100 g
Garlic	30 g
Cooking oil	15 g

Process and application:

Cut the garlic into slices and stir-fry it for a moment in hot cooking oil over fire. Put in the Chinese-date, peanut kernels and 2 bowls of water to decoct until the contents are soft for eating.

Curative properties: Edema caused by different diseases.

Steamed Catfish

Ingredients:

Catfish	100 g

Soy sauce, vinegar, green Chinese onion and ginger dust a little for each

Process and application:

Cut the catfish open, gut it but reserve the mucus on its body, cut it into sections, put it in a plate, season it with flavorings and steam it until it is done.

Curative properties: Edema.

Kelp Cooked with Rice Vinegar

Ingredients:

Fresh kelp	120 g (or dry kelp 60 g)
Rice vinegar	some

Process and application:

Cook the kelp with rice vinegar. It should be avoided by those who suffer from gastric ulcer, duodenal ulcer or hyperhydrochloria.

Curative properties: Edema.

Apricot Kernel and Egg Yolk

Ingredients:

Apricot kernel	6 g
Yolk of hen's egg	1

Process and application:

Pound the apricot kernel and mix it with the yolk well, pour in boiling hot water and take this infusion hot at a draft, once a day. Lie under quilt after eating it. A curative effect will be felt if the patient perspires a bit.

Curative properties: Anasarca.

Millet Gruel with Black Soya-bean and Hen's Eggs

Ingredients:

Black soya-bean	30 g
Millet	90 g
Hen's eggs	2

Process and application:

Cook the above ingredients in water until the eggs are cooked, remove the shells and continue cooking them until the gruel is done. Take the gruel in the same night. A better effect is exerted if the patient perspires a bit after taking the gruel.

Curative properties: Edema.

STRANGURIA (PYELONEPHRITIS, CYSTITIS, URETHRITIS, CALCULUS OF URINARY SYSTEM ETC.)

Bamboo Leaf Tea

Ingredients:

Bamboo leaf	10 g
Tea	5 g

Process and application:

Infuse the above in hot water and take the infusion every day as a drink.

Curative properties: Acute urinary tract infection.

Yangtao Soaked in White Spirit

Ingredients:

Yangtao	250 g
White spirit	500 g

Process and application:

Remove the skin of the yangtao and wash it clean, put it in a jar or bottle full of white spirit, seal the container hermetically, let them infuse there for 20 - 30 days, stir the white spirit once every third day. Take 3 - 15 g of the liquid at a time, twice a day.

Curative properties: Urethral calculus, hemorrhoids.

Soup of Jellyfish and Water Chestnuts

Ingredients:

Jellyfish	200 g
Water chestnuts	9

Process and application:

Add 5 bowls of water to the above ingredients and decoct them until 2 bowls of decoction is left. Take all the soup in one draft.

Curative properties: Difficulty in urination.

Peanut Coat

Ingredients:

Peanut kernels   some

Process and application:

Roast peanut kernels until they are done to obtain half tea-cup of their skins. Pound the skins into fine powder and take an infusion of the powder in hot water.

Curative properties: Cystitis, vesical calculus, senile hematuria.

Leaf Mustard Soup with Hen's Egg

Ingredients:

Fresh leaf mustard	250 g
Hen's egg	1

Process and application:

Wash the leaf mustard clean and cut it into pieces, beat the egg and cook the above ingredients in water to prepare soup. Take the soup at a draft before noon. Keep on eating the soup until the illness is cured.

Curative properties: Calculus of urinary system.

Walnut Kernel Gruel

Ingredients:

Walnut kernel	100 g
Rice	50 g
White sugar	50 g

Process and application:
Pound the walnut kernel, prepare gruel with it and rice and add sugar to it. Take the gruel for supper, for 7 - 20 consecutive days as a course of treatment. It can be taken frequently. It should be avoided by those who have loose stools.

Curative properties: Calculus of urinary tract; constipation.

Lemon Juice

Ingredients:

Fresh lemon	500 g
White sugar	250 g

Process and application:
Wash the lemon clean, cut it into cubes and squeeze its juice out. Add sugar to the juice and keep it under low temperature. Take some of the juice at any time. It can also be taken together with some warm boiled water.

Curative properties: Prevention and cure of calculus of kidney.

NEPHRITIS

Soup of Tortoise and Red Phaseolus Bean

Ingredients:

Tortoise (live)	1 (weight 500 - 700 g)
Red phaseolus bean	50 - 100 g

Process and application:
Keep the tortoise in clear water for 3 to 4 days so that it will vomit all the impurities from its stomach. Cut off its head and discard it. Chop the tortoise and stew it in water along with the red phaseolus bean in an earthenware pot

until the tortoise meat is overdone. Take all the meat and red phaseolus bean with the soup in one day and repeat this for several consecutive days. Salt should be avoided.

Curative properties: Acute nephritis, chronic nephritis.

Soup of Mallard and Garlic

Ingredients:

Mallard   1
Garlic   50 g

Process and application:

Deplume the mallard, gut it, wash it clean, stuff the skinned garlic into it and cook it in water. Take the soup with the meat. The common dosage is one mallard for 2 days. This diet should be repeated several times.

Curative properties: Chronic nephritis.

Sheep Milk

Ingredients:

Fresh sheep milk   400 g

Process and application:

Boil the milk and take it in the morning and in the evening consecutively for a month.

Curative properties: Chronic nephritis.

Soup of Carp and Wax-gourd

Ingredients:

Carp (live)   500 g
Wax-gourd   500 g

Process and application:

Gut the carp and descale it. Peel the wax-gourd and

stew the wax-gourd and carp in clear water. Take the soup with the carp, twice a day.

Curative properties: Early stage and restoration stage of nephritis; infection of urinary system; nephrotic syndrome.

Soup of Peanuts and Broad Bean

Ingredients:

Peanut kernels	120 g
Broad bean	200 g
Brown sugar	50 g

Process and application:

Put the peanut kernels, broad bean and 3 bowls of water in a pot and heat them over soft fire until the decoction becomes brown and somewhat thick. Take the soup after mixing it with brown sugar, twice a day.

Curative properties: Chronic nephritis.

Soup of Red Phaseolus Bean and Wax-gourd

Ingredients:

Red phaseolus bean	150 g
Wax-gourd	250 g

Process and application:

Prepare soup with the above ingredients for eating. The soup is efficacious if taken frequently.

Curative properties: Edema due to chronic nephritis.

Watermelon Juice

Ingredients:

Watermelon	1500 g
White sugar	50 g

Process and application:
Remove the rind and seeds of the watermelon, squeeze the pulp to extract its juice, add sugar to the juice and take it as a drink. This recipe produces good curative effect if it is applied frequently over a period of time.

Curative properties: Edema due to nephritis.

Stewed Beef with Broad Bean

Ingredients:

Broad bean (fresh or dried but softened in water)	250 g
Lean beef	500 g
Table salt	a little

Process and application:
Cut the beef into cubes, add a little salt and stew it with broad bean in water in an earthenware pot until it is very soft.

Curative properties: Acute glomerulonephritis; chronic glomerulonephritis.

Broad Bean Patty

Ingredients:

Broad bean	250 g
Brown sugar	150 g

Process and application:
Soften the broad bean by soaking it in water, remove its skin and cook it in water until it becomes very soft. When it is still hot, mix it with the brown sugar and press it into pulp. Mold it into patties with a bottle cap after it cools off. This recipe can be taken consecutively.

Curative properties: Acute glomerulonephritis; chronic glomerulonephritis.

Soup of Mallard and Wax-gourd

Ingredients:

Mallard	1
Wax-gourd	500 - 1000 g

Process and application:
Kill the mallard, deplume it and gut it. Cut it into cubes. Wash the wax-gourd clean and cut it into thin slices. Stew the above in an earthenware pot until the meat is very soft. Take all the soup (unsalted) with its contents at any time in one day. Repeat this recipe for several consecutive days.

Curative properties: Acute nephritis; anasarca; fever; oliguria. This recipe is also applicable to acute pyelonephritis and hematuria.

DIABETES

Salted Fresh Ginger Soup

Ingredients:

Fresh fresh ginger	2 slices
Table salt	4.5 g
Green tea	6 g

Process and application:
Decoct the above ingredients to prepare 500 ml of soup. Take the soup in several doses.

Curative properties: Thirst with frequent drinking of water; dysphoria with polyuria due to diabetes.

Stewed Crucian Carp with Green Tea

Ingredients:

Crucian carp	500 g

| Green tea | some |

Process and application:
Rid the crucian carp of its gills, gut it but do not descale it, stuff it with the green tea and steam it in a plate until the crucian carp is done. Eat the crucian carp unseasoned and unsalted.

Curative properties: Thirst with frequent drinking of water due to diabetes.

Soup of Spinach Root and White Jellyfungus

Ingredients:
| Spinach root | 100 g |
| White jellyfungus | 10 g |

Process and application:
Decoct the above ingredients in water and take the soup twice a day.

Curative properties: Thirst with frequent drinking of water or hard and dry motions due to diabetes.

Silkworm Chrysalis Decoction

Ingredients:
| Silkworm chrysalises | 10 |

Process and application:
Decoct the above ingredients in water and drink the decoction twice a day.

Curative properties: Polyuria due to diabetes.

Powder of Black Fungus and Hyacinth Bean

Ingredients:
| Black fungus and hyacinth bean | equal amount for each |

Process and application:
Dry the above in sun and, when dry, pound them together into powder. Take an infusion of 9 g powder in hot
water at a time.
Curative properties: Diabetes.

Fried Bamboo Shoot

Ingredients:
Fresh and tender bamboo shoot, soy
    sauce and table salt   some for each
Process and application:
Peel the bamboo shoot and cut it into oblong-formed
slices. Let it infuse in soy sauce for a moment, fish it out,
put it in simmering vegetable oil and fry it until it becomes
yellow.
Curative properties: Diabetes.

Spore-like Efflorescence on Surface
of Wax-gourd

Ingredients:
Wax-gourd   1
Process and application:
Scrape the wax-gourd to collect the spore-like efflorescence from the surface. Take an infusion of the spore-
like efflorescence in hot water. For patient with severe
symptoms this recipe should be taken twice a day for 2 - 3
consecutive days.
Curative properties: Xerostomia, thirst, polydipsia,
polyuria due to diabetes.

Cooked Corn (Maize) Seed

Ingredients:

Corn seeds   500 g

Process and application:

Cook the corn seeds in water until they pop up. Eat them in 4 separate doses, 1000 g making up a course of treatment.

Curative properties: Diabetes.

Hen's Egg White with Ginseng

Ingredients:

Ginseng   6 g

Hen's egg white   1

Process and application:

Pound the ginseng into powder, mix it with egg white well and eat it all in one dose. Take it once a day for 10 consecutive days as a course of treatment.

Curative properties: Diabetes.

Celery Gruel

Ingredients:

Celery (tender stems)   150 g

Rice   100 g

Cooking oil   some

Table salt   some

Process and application:

Wash the celery clean, chop it, cook it along with rice in water and add some oil and salt. The gruel can also be taken warm with seasoning of beef, chicken or fish or taken with bread or cooked rice, once a day for 10 consecutive days as a course of treatment.

Curative properties: Diabetes; hypertension.

Glutinous Rice Gruel with Wolfberry Fruit

Ingredients:

Wolfberry fruit	50 g
Glutinous rice	100 g

Process and application:

Cook gruel with the above ingredients and take the gruel warm once a day. It exerts good effect if taken frequently over a period of time.

Curative properties: Anemia; diabetes.

White Radish Juice

Ingredients:

White radish	any amount

Process and application:

Peel the fresh white radish, wash it clean, chop it and squeeze its juice out. Take 100 - 150 ml of the juice at a time, twice a day for 7 consecutive days as a course of treatment.

Curative properties: Diabetes.

CORONARY HEART DISEASE

Banana Tea

Ingredients:

Banana	50 g
Tea	10 g
Honey	a little

Process and application:

Prepare a cup of hot tea. Peel and smash the banana, mix it and honey in the tea and take one dose of the tea every day.

Curative properties: Coronary heart disease; arteriosclerosis; hypertension.

Tomato Soup with Prickly-ash Peel

Ingredients:

Prickly-ash peel	9 g
Tomato	1500 g
Hen's egg	1

Process and application:

Prepare a bowl of decoction by boiling the prickly-ash peel in water for 20 minutes. Fry the tomato in sesame oil, add the prickly-ash peel decoction, continue heating the mixture and when it boils, beat an egg in it and put in some table salt and gourmet powder. Take this as a soup or take it with bread or cooked rice, once a day for 10 - 20 consecutive days as a course of treatment. Alternatively, take this soup twice a week intermittently for a period of time.

Curative properties: Hypertension; coronary heart disease; anemia.

Gruel of Corn (Maize) Flour

Ingredients:

Corn flour	60 g
Table salt	some

Process and application:

Prepare paste by mixing corn flour and clear water. Boil some water and put the paste bit by bit slowly into the boiling water. Continue heating the water for 15 minutes until they become gruel. Add some oil, salt and other seasonings. Take the gruel for breakfast or supper. It produces good effects if taken regularly.

Curative properties: Coronary heart disease; diabetes.

Kelp

Ingredients:

Kelp (softened in water)   200 g
Sesame oil, sugar and table salt   a little for each

Process and application:

Wash the kelp clean and boil it thoroughly. Dip it in clear water to rinse the mucus off. Drain off the water and cut the kelp into tiny shreds. Heat sesame oil in a pot, when the sesame oil reaches the temperature of 70% of the boiling point, put in the kelp and fry it for a moment. Cover the pot for a moment, take off the lid and continue frying it. When the kelp becomes crisp, strain off the oil and eat the kelp with seasonings of sugar and salt.

Curative properties: Coronary heart disease.

Fried Lean Pork with Onion

Ingredients:

Onion   150 g
Lean pork   50 g
Soy sauce, table salt, oil and
    gourmet powder   some for each

Process and application:

Put a little oil in a pot and heat it until it reaches the temperature of 80% of the boiling point. Put in the pork to fry, add the onion to it and continue frying them for a moment. Add flavorings and continue frying it for a moment.

Curative properties: Prevention of atherosclerosis.

Soup of Tremella and Black Fungus

Ingredients:

Tremella	10 g
Black fungus	10 g
Crystal sugar	5 g

Process and application:

Soften the tremella and black fungus in warm water, put them in a bowl with some water and crystal sugar, steam them for one hour and take the soup with its contents.

Curative properties: Angiosclerosis; hypertension; coronary heart disease.

Raw Hawthorn Fruit Preserved in Honey

Ingredients:

Raw hawthorn fruit	500 g
Honey	250 g

Process and application:

Wash the raw hawthorn fruits clean, remove their stems and stones, cook them in water until they are 70 percent done. As the decoction is about to dry, put in honey and continue cooking them over slow fire until the decoction boils down to jelly. Put this in a bottle for later use. Take the jelly regularly.

Curative properties: Angina pectoris due to coronary heart disease.

Soup of Knuckle of a Pig with Pickled Mustard Tuber

Ingredients:

| Knuckle of a pig | 250 g |
| Pickled mustard tuber | 25 g |

Process and application:

Remove the skin and fat from the knuckle of a pig, stew it in water and when the knuckle becomes very soft, tear it into pieces, add the shreds of pickled mustard tuber and continue heating the soup until it boils. Take this soup after seasoning it with gourmet powder.

Curative properties: Revivification, antishock; it is applicable to myocardiac infarction with stable symptoms.

HYPERTENSION

Decoction of Celery and Chinese-date

Ingredients:

| Celery | 350 - 700 g |
| Chinese-date | 100 - 200 g |

Process and application:

Decoct the above ingredients and take the decoction in 3 separate dose every day.

Curative properties: Hypertension.

Gruel with Chrysanthemum Flower

Ingredients:

Chrysanthemum flower	10 g
Rice	50 g
Crystal sugar	some

Process and application:

Prepare gruel with chrysanthemum flower and washed rice and add crystal sugar to it when the gruel is about to be done. Continue cooking the gruel until the rice is very soft. Frequent application of this recipe is helpful.

Curative properties: Hypertension.

Celery Soup with Sugar

Ingredients:

Celery	500 g
White sugar	50 g

Process and application:

Wash the celery (with its roots and leaves) clean and decoct it for 30 minutes. Add some sugar to the soup and take it twice a day.

Curative properties: Hypertension.

Decoction of Lemon and Water Chestnut

Ingredients:

Lemon	1
Water chestnuts	10

Process and application:

Decoct the above ingredients in water. Drink the decoction and/or eat its contents. It remains effective even if taken regularly.

Curative properties: Hypertension; myocardiac infarction.

Decoction of Chinese-date and Root of Celery

Ingredients:

Chinese-date and root of celery   some for each

Process and application:

Wash the above ingredients clean and decoct them in water. Take some of the decoction frequently.

Curative properties: Hypertension.

Celery Juice with Honey

Ingredients:

Celery and honey   some for each

Process and application:

Extract the juice of fresh celery, add an equal amount of honey to the juice, heat it and mix it well. Take 40 ml of the juice at a time, 3 times a day.

Curative properties: Hypertension.

Hawthorn Fruit Decoction with Sugar

Ingredients:

Fresh hawthorn fruits   10

Sugar   30 g

Process and application:

Pound the hawthorn fruits and decoct them with sugar until they become very soft. Take the decoction with its contents once a day.

Curative properties: Hypertension.

Sunflower Seed with Celery Root Extract

Ingredients:

Raw sunflower seed   50 g

Celery root   100 g

Process and application:

Husk the sunflower seeds and eat them along with a cup of juice extracted from the pounded celery root. Take it at a draft.

Curative properties: Hypertension.

Peanut Kernels Soaked in Vinegar

Ingredients:
Raw peanut kernels and vinegar   some for each
Process and application:
Put half a bowl of raw peanut kernels (unskinned) into a bowlful of vinegar and let the peanut kernels infuse in the vinegar for 7 days. Eat 10 peanut kernels in the morning and 10 in the evening every day. Resume taking it several days later after the blood pressure is brought down.
Curative properties: Hypertension.

Decoction of Kelp and Mung Bean

Ingredients:

Kelp	150 g
Mung bean	150 g
Brown sugar	150 g

Process and application:
Soak the kelp in water, wash it clean and cut it into pieces. Wash the mung bean clean. Cook the kelp and mung bean until they become very soft. Take the decoction with brown sugar twice a day. This diet can be taken repeatedly.
Curative properties: Hyperlipemia; hypertension.

Yangtao

Ingredients:
Fresh yangtao   some
Process and application:
Wash it clean and eat it. Alternatively, squeeze its juice out for drinking. This recipe is helpful in preventing

carcinogenic amine nitrite from building up in human body.

Curative properties: Hypertension; angiocardiopathy; hepatosplenomegaly; it helps to bring down blood-lipid, cholesterol and triglyceride.

Infusion of Chrysanthemum Flower, Sophora Flower and Green Tea

Ingredients:

Chrysanthemum flower	3 g
Sophora flower	3 g
Green tea	3 g

Process and application:
Put the above ingredients in a mug, pour in hot boiled water, cover the mug and let them infuse in water for 5 minutes. Drink the infusion at short intervals, several doses a day.

Curative properties: Hypertension.

Oolong Tea with Chrysanthemum Flower

Ingredients:

Chrysanthemum flower	10 g
Oolong tea (or Dragon Well tea)	3 g

Process and application:
Soak the tea in hot boiled water. The tea should not be very strong, else it will cause insomnia and speed the heartbeat.

Curative properties: Hypertension.

Green Tea with Apple Skin

Ingredients:

Green tea	1 g
Apple skin	50 g
Honey	25 g

Process and application:

Wash the apple skin clean and heat it in 450 ml of water. After the water boils, continue decocting it for 5 minutes. Add some honey and green tea. Divide the whole decoction into 3 separate doses and take one dose(warm) a day.

Curative properties: Hypertension.

Tea with Lotus Plumule

Ingredients:

| Green tea | 1 g |
| Lotus plumule (dry) | 3 g |

Process and application:

Put the lotus plumule with green tea in a cup, pour in hot water, cover the cup and leave them infuse for 5 minutes. Take the infusion after meal. When the first extract is about to be drunk off, leave a little decoction in the cup and add hot water to get another extract for drinking, until the extract becomes tasteless.

Curative properties: Hypertension.

APOPLEXY (CEREBROVASCULAR ACCIDENT)

Cherry Soaked in White Spirit

Ingredients:

| Fresh cherry | 200 g |
| White spirit | 500 g |

Process and application:

Sift the cherries from impurities and wash them clean. Infuse them in white spirit in a hermetically sealed jar for 15 - 20 days and stir the white spirit every other or third day. Take 15 - 30 g of the infusion at a time, twice a day.

Curative properties: Paralysis.

Black Soyabean Infused in Yellow Rice or Millet Wine

Ingredients:

Black soyabean (small)	some
Yellow rice or millet wine	some

Process and application:

Roast the black soyabean until it becomes brown, infuse it in half cup of yellow rice or millet wine. Take it hot and lie under quilt. A curative effect will be felt when the patient perspires a bit.

Curative properties: Affection by cold after delivery; tetraplegia; facial hemiparalysis.

Rooster's Blood

Ingredients:

Rooster's blood	some

Process and application:

Draw fresh blood from a rooster with a syringe and smear the warm blood (if it is cold, warm it) on the cheek where the symptom is slight.

Curative properties: Facial hemiparalysis due to apoplexy.

Carp's Blood

Ingredients:

Fresh carp's blood and white sugar
                                    equal amount for each
Process and application:
Mix the above well and smear the mixture on the left side if the right side of face is paralyzed, and vice versa.

Curative properties: Facial hemiparalysis due to apoplexy.

Shell of Hen's Egg Infused in Yellow Rice or Millet Wine

Ingredients:

Shell of hen's egg	120 g
Yellow rice or millet wine	some

Process and application:
Roast the egg-shell until it becomes yellow, pound it into fine powder and take an infusion of 6 g powder in yellow rice or millet wine at a time.

Curative properties: Numbness of the extremities; tenany.

Mashed Garlic

Ingredients:

Garlic	2 cloves

Process and application:
Skin the garlic, smash it and smear the mash on the root of the teeth.

Curative properties: Aphasia from apoplexy.

Black Soyabean Jelly

Ingredients:

Black soyabean	some

Process and application:
Wash the black soyabean clean, cook it in water until the decoction boils down to jelly. Keep it in the mouth for a moment and swallow it down. Take it several times a day.

Curative properties: Aphasia from apoplexy.

Sesame Seed Pill

Ingredients:

Black sesame seed	some
Yellow rice or millet wine	a little

Process and application:
Wash the sesame seed clean, repeatedly steam it 3 times, dry it in sun and when dry, roast it and pound it into fine powder. Roll pills by mixing it with honey. Each pill should weigh 10 g. Take one pill at a time with warm yellow rice or millet wine, 3 times a day.

Curative properties: Hemiparalysis due to apoplexy.

PARASITOSIS

Areca Seed

Ingredients:

Areca seed	9 g

Process and application:
Pound the areca seed into fine powder and take an infusion of 3 g powder in warm boiled water at a time, 3 times a day.

Curative properties: Infantile cestodiasis. It also kills roundworm and pinworm.

Green Plum in Yellow Rice or Millet Wine

Ingredients:

Green plum	30 g
Yellow rice or millet wine	100 ml

Process and application:

Rid the green plum of the impurities, wash it clean and soak it in yellow rice or millet wine in a mug. Put the mug in a steamer to steam it for 20 minutes. Take 10 - 30 ml of the liquid at a time, twice a day.

Curative properties: Abdominal pain due to roundworm.

Patty of Chinese Chive Root and Egg

Ingredients:

Chinese chive root	120 g
Hen's egg	1

Process and application:

Pound the Chinese chive root to extract its juice. Beat the egg, mix it with the juice, make a patty with the mixture and steam it until it is done. Take it on an empty stomach, for 3 consecutive days.

Curative properties: Roundworm.

Egg Fried in Soyabean Oil

Ingredients:

Soyabean oil	some
Hen's egg	1

Process and application:

Beat the egg and fry it in soyabean oil until it becomes a patty. Apply it to the anus before sleep for 7 consecutive days.

Curative properties: Oxyuriasis.

Peach Leaf Pill

Ingredients:

Peach leaves (the fresh leaves at the
  tip of boughs)   dozens
Chinese chives   a handful

Process and application:

Cut the Chinese chives into pieces and pound it to extract its juice. Pulp the peach leaves, mix them with Chinese chives juice and knead the mixture. Roll the mixture into pills in size to a stone of Chinese-date. Insert one pill into the child's anus after it goes to sleep and 15 minutes later pinworms will come out and attach themselves to the pill. Throw away the pill immediately and catch the pinworms around the anus. Repeat this for several days until no pinworm is found. If peach leaves are not available, tender Chinese chives may be a substitute.

Curative properties: Pruritus ani due to oxyuriasis.

Sesame Oil with Fried Prickly-ash Peel

Ingredients:

Prickly-ash peel   12 g
Sesame oil   60 ml

Process and application:

Heat the sesame oil in a pot until no smoke is seen, put in the prickly-ash peel and fried it until it becomes light brown. Remove the pot from the fire, fish out the prickly-ash peel and drink all the oil in one dose when it becomes lukewarm.

Curative properties: Pain around the navel or intestinal obstruction due to roundworm.

Warning: This recipe is not applicable to the cases of lasting intestinal obstruction with obvious complications of toxicosis or intestinal necrosis.

MALARIAL DISEASE

Hen's Egg White Mixed in White Spirit

Ingredients:

Hen's egg	1
White spirit	20 ml

Process and application:

Beat the egg to obtain the egg white, mix the egg white in white spirit and take the mixture at a draft. For purpose of prevention, take it once a week, for 2 or 3 consecutive weeks; for purpose of cure, double the dosage and take it at a draft 2 hours before the attack.

Curative properties: Malarial disease.

Soft-shelled Turtle Stewed in Lard

Ingredients:

Soft-shelled turtle	1
Lard	20 g
Table salt	a little

Process and application:

Kill the soft-shelled turtle, gut it and cut it into cubes. Put the cubes along with its crust and the meat around the crust into a basin, add lard, clear water and a little salt, heat them by leaving the basin in boiling water for 4 hours until the meat is done. Take it warm.

Curative properties: Persistent chronic malaria.

Honey with White Spirit

Ingredients:

Honey   15 - 30 g

White spirit   some

Process and application:

Warm the white spirit a bit, pour it in honey and mix them well. Take it half an hour before the attack of malarial disease. If the exact time of attack is unknown, take this recipe 3 times in the day of attack.

Curative properties: Malarial disease.

Broth of Bone from Carcass of a Sheep

Ingredients:

Bone from carcass of a sheep   250 g

Process and application:

Wash the bone clean, smash it and boil it in water. Take the broth 3 hours before the attack of malarial disease.

Curative properties: Malarial disease.

Soup of Mutton and Soft-shelled Turtle

Ingredients:

Mutton, soft-shelled turtle, sugar,

     table salt   some for each

Process and application:

Cut the mutton into small pieces, head the soft-shelled turtle, gut it and remove its feet. Stew the mutton and turtle in water with sugar and salt. Take one bowl of the soup and eat the meat every day.

Curative properties: Malarial disease.

Gallbladder of a Chicken

Ingredients:

Gallbladder of a chicken	1

Process and application:

Take a fresh gallbladder of a chicken from a newly-killed hen or rooster and swallow it down. Take one gall-bladder every other day. The illness is likely to be cured after 3 or 4 chicken gallbladders have been taken.

Curative properties: Malarial disease.

Red Phaseolus Bean with Paradise Fish of China

Ingredients:

Red phaseolus bean	100 g
Paradise fish of China	1
Chinese-dates	10
Dried tangerine peel	5 g
Fresh ginger	50 g

Process and application:

Wash the red phaseolus bean clean. Gut the paradise fish of China. Cook the red phaseolus bean and paradise fish of China with table salt, dried tangerine peel, Chinese-dates and fresh ginger until they become very soft. Take it at one draft.

Curative properties: Malaria tertiana; quartan malaria or persistent malarial disease.

NEURASTHENIA; PALPITATION ; INSOMNIA

Mulberry Decoction

Ingredients:

Mulberry   15 g

Process and application:

Decoct the mulberry in water and take the decoction as a drink.

Curative properties: Insomnia; palpitation; amnesia.

Decoction of Longan Aril and Root of American Ginseng

Ingredients:

Longan aril   30 g
Root of American ginseng   6 g
White sugar   a little

Process and application:

Soak the root of American ginseng in water and cut it into pieces. Rid the longan aril of the impurities and wash it clean. Put them in a basin, add some sugar and clear water and steam them for 40 - 50 minutes. Take the decoction with its contents once in the morning and once in the evening.

Curative properties: Insomnia; palpitation; amnesia.

Glutinous Rice Gruel with Wheat and Chinese-date

Ingredients:

Wheat   50 g
Glutinous rice   100 g
Chinese-dates   5
Dried longan pulp   15 g
White sugar   20 g

Process and application:

Wash the wheat clean, soak it in hot water until it becomes soft, boil it in water. Strain off the decoction and cook washed glutinous rice along with stoned Chinese-dates and dried longan pulp in the decoction until they become gruel. Take the gruel hot after adding some sugar, 2 or 3 times a day for 4 - 5 consecutive days as a course of treatment.

Curative properties: Insomnia; night sweat.

Gruel with Wild Jujuba Seed

Ingredients:

Wild jujuba seed (raw or roasted)	30 g
Rice	100 g

Process and application:

Pestle the wild jujuba seed and decoct it in water until it becomes a thick decoction. Prepare gruel with washed rice. When the gruel is half done, add the wild jujuba seed decoction and continue cooking the gruel until it is done. Take the gruel warm every night.

Curative properties: Arrhythmia; spontaneous perspiration; night sweat; insomnia.

Yolk Cream

Ingredients:

Hen's eggs	100

Process and application:

Boil the eggs and shell them. Obtain the yolks and stew them over soft fire until 500 g cream is extracted. Take a spoonful of the cream at a time, twice a day. Take it consecutively.

Curative properties: Arrhythmia.

Decoction of Chinese-date with Cow's Liver (or Sheep Liver)

Ingredients:

Cow's liver (or sheep liver)   250 g
Chinese-dates   15

Process and application:

Chop the cow's liver (or sheep liver) and cook it with Chinese-date in water.

Curative properties: Palpitation with lassitude.

Cooked Hen's Egg with Wolfberry Fruit

Ingredients:

Wolfberry fruit   20 g
Chinese-dates   6
Hen's eggs   2

Process and application:

Cooked the above ingredients in water and take them once a day.

Curative properties: Dizziness with dim sight; palpitation; amnesia; lassitude.

Steamed Hen's Egg with Ginseng

Ingredients:

Ginseng   3 g
Hen's egg   1

Process and application:

Grind the ginseng into powder and mix it with the egg. Steam the mixture and take it at a draft. Take it once a day, for 15 consecutive days as a course of treatment.

Curative properties: Loss of mental vitality in old age.

Steamed Egg with Dried Longan Pulp

Ingredients:

Dried longan pulp	6 pcs
Hen's egg	1
White sugar	some

Process and application:

Beat the egg in a bowl but do not stir it. Add sugar and steam the egg until it is half done. Stuff the dried longan pulp into the yolk and continue steaming the egg until it is done. Take the egg as a snack, once a day. This recipe is to be taken regularly.

Curative properties: Palpitation; amnesia; insomnia.

Honeyed Milk with Yolk

Ingredients:

Hen's egg	1
Milk	250 g
Honey	30 g

Process and application:

Beat the egg in a bowl, pour in hot boiled milk, stir it slowly with a spoon and then add honey. Take it hot, once a day for 10 consecutive days as course of treatment. It can be taken regularly.

Curative properties: Neurasthenia; hypomnesis; insomnia.

Soup of Quail's Egg and Shelled Fresh Shrimps

Ingredients:

Quail's eggs	10

Shelled fresh shrimps	50 g
Lean pork	50 g
Hen's egg white	1
Table salt and starch	some for each

Process and application:

Mix the shelled fresh shrimps, minced lean pork, salt, starch and egg white. Cook the quail's eggs, shell them and cut them each into halves and dust some starch over them. Smear the quail's egg with the mixture of shelled fresh shrimps and other ingredients. Arrange the eggs on a plate and steam the plate with eggs over strong fire for 5 minutes. Boil a big bowlful of water and put in chopped vegetables, some salt and the steamed quail's egg to prepare soup. Eat the soup with bread or rice, or take it for supper.

Curative properties: Neurasthenia.

SEMINAL EMISSION; IMPOTENCE; PREMATURE EJACULATION

Chinese Chive Seed Decoction

Ingredients:

| Chinese chive seed | 20 pcs |

Process and application:

Decoct the Chinese chive seed in salt water and take the decoction as a drink.

Curative properties: Seminal emission.

Prawn Soaked in White Spirit

Ingredients:

| Prawn | 2 |
| White spirit | 250 g |

Process and application:
Wash prawn clean and let them infuse in white spirit in a covered jar for 7 days. Take 10 - 15 g of the liquid at a time, twice a day.

Curative properties: Hypogonadism; impotence.

Chinese Chive Seed with White Spirit

Ingredients:

Chinese chive seed	100 g
White spirit	75 g

Process and application:
Bake the Chinese chive seed until it dries, pound it into powder and take an infusion of all the powder in white spirit in 3 separate doses within one day.

Curative properties: Nocturnal emission; spermatorrhea or spermaturia.

Gruel with Walnut Kernel and Wolfberry Fruit

Ingredients:

Walnut kernel	50 g
Wolfberry fruit	15 g
Rice	some

Process and application:
Pound the walnut kernel, wash the rice clean and cook them along with the wolfberry fruit until they become gruel. Taken the gruel with bread or cooked rice regularly.

Curative properties: Seminal abnormity; cloudy urine.

Gruel with Chinese Chive Seed

Ingredients:

| Chinese chive seed | 25 g |
| Rice | 100 g |

Process and application:
Wrap the Chinese chive seeds in gauze and decoct them in water. Add rice to the decoction to cook until they become gruel. Take the gruel twice a day.

Curative properties: Enuresis; seminal emission.

Stewed Kidney of a Pig with Walnut Kernel

Ingredients:
| Pig kidneys | 2 |
| Walnut kernel | 30 g |

Process and application:
Stew the above ingredients together until they are soft for eating.

Curative properties: Premature ejaculation.

Walnut Kernel Emulsion

Ingredients:
| Walnut kernel | 200 g |
| Cooking oil, sugar | some |

Process and application:
Fry the walnut kernels in oil until they become crisp. Grind them with sugar into an emulsion or electuary. Take all the emulsion in separate doses in 1 or 2 days. Alternatively, prepare gruel with the rice and 100 g walnut kernels. Take some of the gruel with sugar.

Curative properties: Premature ejaculation.

Glutinous Rice Gruel with Lotus Root

Ingredients:

103

| Fresh lotus root | several sections |
| Glutinous rice, crystal sugar | some |

Process and application:

Dissolve the crystal sugar in warm water and leave the glutinous rice soak in the water for half a day. Wash the lotus root clean and rid it of the joints, fill the holes inside the lotus root with glutinous rice and cook it until it is done. Take 1 or 2 sections of the lotus root every day. Overdose produces no negative effect.

Curative properties: Nocturnal emission; vexation.

Decoction of Lichee and Lotus Seed

Ingredients:

Dry lichee	30 g
Lotus seed	50 g
White sugar	50 g

Process and application:

Boil the lichee and lotus seed in water and add some sugar. Take the decoction with bread or cooked rice, once a day, for 7 consecutive days as a course of treatment.

Curative properties: Impotence.

Eel Soup

Ingredients:

Eel	1
Coriander, table salt and	
pepper powder	some for each

Process and application:

Cut the eel into cakes after washing it clean and gutting it. Fry it with salt in oil until it is half done, add some clear water, cover the pot and continue cooking it over strong fire for 20 minutes. Move it over to slow fire, continue heating it for half an hour and season it with the flavorings. Take it with bread or cooked rice, or take it for breakfast or supper. Continuous application of this recipe is helpful.

Curative properties: Impotence; pulmonary tuberculosis; gastric ulcer.

Recipes for Surgical Diseases

SKIN AND EXTERNAL DISEASES

Tea Leaves (for External Application)

Ingredients:

Tea leaves   any amount

Process and application:

Infuse the tea leaves in water to soften them and apply them to the affected part. When the leaves get dry, replace them with wet ones.

Curative properties: Innominate inflammatory swelling; bite by dog; burn.

Garlic Cooked in White Spirit

Ingredients:

Garlic   250 g

White spirit   500 g

Process and application:

Pulp the garlic and boil it in 500 g white spirit until the garlic becomes very soft. Store it in a bottle for later use. Take 30 ml white spirit(together with the garlic pulp) at a time. The curative effect will be achieved on perspiration of the patient.

Curative properties: Spasm due to skin and external diseases with affection of wind.

Loofah Juice

Ingredients:

Fresh loofah   1

Process and application:

Cut the loofah into pieces and pound it to extract its juice. Apply the juice to the affected part at short intervals.

Curative properties: Non-healing of boils; deep opening of sore.

Stewed Pig's Trotters with Green Chinese Onion

Ingredients:

Green Chinese onion	100 g
Pig's trotters	4
Table salt	some

Process and application:

Wash the pig's trotters clean, cut openings in their skin and stew them with green Chinese onion (cut into sections) and some salt in water until the water boils. Move them to slow fire and continue cooking them until the meat is very soft. Take the meat with the soup in 2 separate doses every day.

Curative properties: Skin and external diseases with swelling pain.

Hen's Egg Shell with Slaked Lime

Ingredients:

Slaked lime	15 g
Hen's egg shells	5

Process and application:

Fill the egg-shells with slaked lime and roast them over fire. Ground them into power, mix them with sesame oil and apply the mixture to the affected parts.

Curative properties: Early stage of furuncle.

Cream of Dried Gypsum Powder and Egg White

Ingredients:

Dried gypsum powder	30 g
Hen's egg white	some

Process and application:

Mix the above ingredients into a cream and apply it to the affected parts, 2 or 3 times a day.

Curative properties: Furuncle without suppuration.

Sesame Oil and Hen's Eggs

Ingredients:

Hen's eggs	3
Sesame oil	15 ml
Yellow rice or millet wine	some

Process and application:

Boil the sesame oil in a pot, beat the eggs in the pot and fry them until they are done. Take the eggs with yellow rice or millet wine.

Curative properties: Nail-like boil and carbuncle.

Bulb of Chinese Onion with Sesame Oil

Ingredients:

Sesame oil and bulb of Chinese onion (the part above the root)	some for each

Process and application:

Heat the sesame oil until it boils and smoke rises, pour it out of the pot and leave it cool. Dip the bulb of Chinese onion in the sesame oil and apply it to the affected parts. An application lasts 20 - 30 minutes. Use this recipe for 3 consecutive days.

Curative properties: Colliculitis.

Instant Gruel of Mung Bean, Glutinous Rice and Wheat

Ingredients:

Mung bean	30 g
Glutinous rice	30 g
Wheat	30 g

Process and application:

Roast the above ingredients in a pan until they are done. Pound them into powder and mix them well. Take a thick infusion of 30 g powder in hot boiled water.

Curative properties: Skin or external diseases with pyogenic infections.

Fresh Fig

Ingredients:

Fresh fig   some

Process and application:

Wash the fig clean, pulp it, apply it to the affected parts and fix it with bandage. Renew it once a day.

Curative properties: Ulcer of lower limb.

Soy Bean Paste

Ingredients:

Soy bean   some

Process and application:

Wash the soy bean clean, cook it until it swells and is half done. Fish it out and stir it to rid it of the skin. Pound it into paste. Apply the paste to the affected part and fix it with bandage. Renew it once a day.

Curative properties: Ulcer of lower limb.

Beef Soup with Chinese-date

Ingredients:

Beef	250 g
Chinese-dates	10

Process and application:

Cut the beef into small pieces and stew it with the Chinese-dates in water over slow fire. Take it twice a day.

Curative properties: This recipe speeds the healing of the wound and therefore is very suitable for the patient after operation.

Live Crab

Ingredients:

Live crab	1

Process and application:

Pound the live crab and apply the mash on the affected part.

Curative properties: Persistent scabies and exudative dermatitis.

Ointment of Lard and Egg Yolk

Ingredients:

Lard and egg yolk	2 portions to 1

Process and application:

Mix one portion of the cooked yolk and two portions of melted lard (sifted from dregs) into an ointment. Put it in a cup and stir it. Heat it over fire and stir it until the lard bulbs and becomes very thin. Wash the affected part with 0.1% bromogeramine, apply the ointment to the affected part and bandage it.

Curative properties: Persistent chronic ulcer.

Tobacco Leaf and Camphor

Ingredients:

Tobacco leaf	5 g
Camphor	3 g
Honey	some

Process and application:

Cut the tobacco leaf into slices and roast it until it becomes dry. Grind it into dust and mix the dust with camphor and honey into a paste. Apply the paste to the affected part.

Curative properties: Carbuncle of the nape.

SCROFULA (TUBERCULOSIS OF LYMPH NODE)

Celery Gruel

Ingredients:

Celery	100 g
Rice	200 g
Table salt, gourmet powder	some for each

Process and application:

Wash the celery (with its root) clean, cook it with washed rice in water over strong fire until the water boils. Continue cooking them over slow fire until the rice is very soft. Add salt and gourmet powder to the gruel and take it for a meal.

Curative properties: Scrofula; mumps.

Paste of Chinese Yam and Castor-seeds

Ingredients:

Fresh Chinese yam	1 piece
Castor-seeds	3

Process and application:

Wash the above clean, pulp them and mix them well into paste. Apply the paste to the affected part twice a day.

Curative properties: Thyroid enlargement; scrofula with hard, red swelling.

Soup of Laver and Dry Mussel

Ingredients:

Laver	15 g
Dry mussel	60 g

Process and application:

Wash the laver clean and soak the dry mussel in clear water. Cook the above in water in an earthenware pot over soft fire. Eat the soup with its contents when it is done.

Curative properties: Early stage of common thyroid enlargement.

Kelp Preserved in Brown Sugar

Ingredients:

Kelp and brown sugar	some for each

Process and application:

Wash the kelp clean and rinse sand off it. Cook it in

water until it is soft, fish it out and cut it into thin shreds. Mix it with brown sugar in a bowl and leave it for half a day. This recipe is effective if taken regularly.

Curative properties: Thyroid enlargement.

Cotton-seed Powder

Ingredients:

Cotton-seed, white spirit and
    granulated sugar   some for each

Process and application:

Parch the cotton-seed and when dry, skin it. Mix it with white spirit and roast it until it is brown. Pestle it and grind it into fine powder and add granulated sugar to it. Take 10 g of the powder at a time, 3 times a day, for a month as a course of treatment.

Curative properties: Tuberculosis of lymph node.

Powder of Glutinous Rice and Sophora Flower

Ingredients:

Glutinous rice	50 g
Sophora flower	100 g

Process and application:

Roast the above ingredients until they are yellow, grind them into powder and take 15 g of the powder in the morning on an empty stomach.

Curative properties: Scrofula.

Soup of Snail and Pork

Ingredients:

Fresh snail	100 g (or dried snail 50 g)
Lean portk	150 g

113

Table salt and soy sauce a little for each
Process and application:
Wash the snail clean and kill them in hot water. Pick out the meat and wash the meat clean. Cook soup with the pork and the snail meat. Take the soup with its contents.

Curative properties: Tuberculosis of lymph node, chronic lymphadenitis.

HEMORRHOIDS; ANAL FISTULA

Decoction of Black Fungus and Black Sesame Seed

Ingredients:

Black fungus	60 g
Black sesame seed	15 g
Sugar	some

Process and application:
Wash a pot clean and heat it over fire. When it is hot, put in the 30 g black fungus to roast until it turns from grey to black. Take it out and put it in a bowl. Roast the sesame seed until a bit of its flavor emits. Add 1500 ml water and cook the sesame and all the black fungus in it for about 30 minutes. Sift the decoction through double layer gauze into a container. Take 100 - 200 ml of the decoction with 20 - 25 g sugar at a time. Regular application of this decoction produces good curative effect.

Curative properties: Hematochezia due to hemorrhoids.

Gruel with Spinach

Ingredients:

Spinach	250 g

114

| Rice | 250 g |
| Table salt and gourmet powder | some for each |

Process and application:
Wash the spinach (with root) clean and cut it into sections. Cook washed rice in water over strong fire until it boils, continue heating it over slow fire until it becomes gruel. Put the spinach into the gruel, heat it for a moment and add salt and gourmet powder to it before eating.

Curative properties: Bleeding due to hemorrhoids.

Pork Soup with Sophora Flower

Ingredients:
| Lean portk | 100 g |
| Sophora flower | 50 g |

Process and application:
Cook soup with the above ingredients. Take the soup once a day.

Curative properties: Hemorrhoids.

Pomegranate Rind Decoction

Ingredients:
| Pomegranate rind | 60 g |
| Alum | 15 g |

Process and application:
Decoct the above ingredients in water. Apply the decoction hot to the affected part, once in the morning and once in the evening.

Curative properties: Proctoptosis.

Chinese-date Stewed in Mature Vinegar

Ingredients:

115

| Mature vinegar | 250 g |
| Chinese-date | 120 g |

Process and application:

Wash the Chinese-date clean and boil it in mature vinegar until the mature vinegar is dry. Take all the cooked Chinese-date in 2 or 3 seperate doses.

Curative properties: Persistent proctoptosis.

Pigskin Boiled in Yellow Rice or Millet Wine

Ingredients:

Fresh pigskin	150 g
Yellow rice or millet wine	300 ml
Brown sugar	50 g

Process and application:

Cook the pigskin in equal amount of water and yellow rice or millet wine over slow fire until the pigskin is very soft. Add the brown sugar and take the soup with its contents in 2 seperate doses in one day. This recipe can be taken for several consecutive days.

Curative properties: Bleeding due to internal hemorrhoid.

Aubergine Powder

Ingredients:

| Aubergine | some |

Process and application:

Cut the aubergine into slices, roast it to charcoal and pound it into fine powder. Take an infusion of 10 g of the powder at a time, 3 time a day, for 10 consecutive days.

Curative properties: Bleeding due to internal hemorrhoid.

Stewed Bananas

Ingredients:

Bananas (unpeeled)   2

Process and application:

Stew the bananas in water. Take the soup with its contents.

Curative properties: Bleeding due to internal hemorrhoid.

Red Phaseolus Bean Cooked in Vinegar

Ingredients:

Red phaseolus bean   500 g

Vinegar and white spirit   some for each

Process and application:

Wash the red phaseolus bean clean, boil it in vinegar until it is done, fish it out and dry it in sun. Soak it in white spirit until all the liquid is absorbed. Dry it and pound it into powder. Take an infusion of 5 g of the power in white spirit at a time, twice a day.

Curative properties: Bleeding due to internal hemorrhoid.

Soup of Crucian Carp and Chinese Chives

Ingredients:

Crucian carp   1 (weight: about 200 g)

Chinese chives   some

Soy sauce and table salt   a little for each

Process and application:

Gut the crucian carp but do not descale it. Wash it clean and fill it with Chinese chives. Put it in a bowl with soy sauce and salt, cover the bowl and steam it for half an hour. Take the soup with the contents once a day.

Curative properties: Hemorrhoid complicated by anal fistula; internal hemorrhoid; external hemorrhoids.

Black Fungus Soup

Ingredients:

Black fungus   30 g

Process and application:

Rid the black fungus of the impurities, wash it clean and stew it in a little water over slow fire until it becomes thick soup. Take the soup at a draft.

Curative properties: Internal hemorrhoid; external hemorrhoids.

PAROTITIS

Soup of Soy Bean and Mung Bean

Ingredients:

Mung bean   160 g
Soy bean   130 g
Brown sugar   120 g

Process and application:

Cook the above ingredients in water until they become very soft. Take any amount of the soup at any time.

Curative properties: Malaise due to red swelling caused by parotitis in children.

Paste of Mature Vinegar and Garlic

Ingredients:

Mature vinegar and garlic (skinned)

equal amount for each

Process and application:

Pulp the above ingredients together to make a paste and apply it fresh to the affected part, 1 - 3 times a day. Repeat this until the disease is cured.

Curative properties: Parotitis; ordinary carbuncle and swelling.

Secretion of Earthworm

Ingredients:

Big earthworms	several
Granulated sugar	a little

Process and application:

Wash the earthworms clean and put them in a clean bowl. Add granulated sugar and after a while of wriggling, the earthworms will secrete white mucus. Apply the secretion to the affected part and renew it when it dries. Repeat this until the disease is cured.

Curative properties: Early stage of acute, epidemic parotitis.

Paste of Red Phaseolus Bean and Egg White

Ingredients:

Red phaseolus beans	70
Hen's egg white	1

Process and application:

Pound the red phaseolus beans into powder and mix the powder with the egg white. Apply this paste to the affected part.

Curative properties: Parotitis.

Gruel from Mung Bean and the Heart of Peking Cabbage

Ingredients:

Mung bean	100 g
Hearts of Peking cabbage	3

Process and application:

Wash the mung bean clean, cook it in some water until it becomes soft. Add the hearts of Peking cabbage and continue cooking them for 20 minutes. Take the gruel in 2 seperate doses in one day, for 4 or 5 consecutive days.

Curative properties: Parotitis in children.

Hen's Egg with Jew's Ear

Ingredients:

Hen's egg	1
Jew's ear	15 g

Process and application:

Beat the egg and mix it with Jew's ear (dried and pounded into powder). Feed this mixture to the suffering child in 3 - 4 seperate doses in one day.

Curative properties: Parotitis in children.

Pepper Powder

Ingredients:

Pepper powder	1 g
Flour	8 g

Process and application:

Mix the above ingredients and warm water into paste, put it on gauze and apply the gause to the affected part. Renew it once a day, for 3 consecutive days.

Curative properties: Epidemic parotitis.

FROSTBITE

Chili Pepper Soaked in White Spirit

Ingredients:

Chili pepper	10 - 15 g
White spirit	some

Process and application:

Shred the chili pepper and let it infuse in white spirit for 10 days. Strain off the liquid and apply it to the red and swollen part or itching part, 3 - 5 times a day. Apply it lightly so as not to scratch the skin.

Curative properties: Swell, red and itching due to early stage of frostbite.

Old Loofah with Lard

Ingredients:

Old loofah and lard	some for each

Process and application:

Burn the old loofah until it is reduced to ashe. Mix the ashe with lard and apply the mixture to the affected part.

Curative properties: Frostbite in hand or foot.

Chili Powder with Vaseline

Ingredients:

Dried chili pepper	2 portions
Vaseline	8 portions

Process and application:

Roast the chili pepper in a pot until it becomes dry. Grind it into powder and mix the powder with vaseline.

Curative properties: This recipe can prevent frostbite. It is applicable to the helix, hand's back, heel, etc. to those who work outdoors in cold winter.

Carrot

Ingredients:

Carrot   1

Process and application:

Wash it clean, peel it and broil it over fire until it is done. Repeatedly rub the affected part lightly with it.

Curative properties: Frostbite.

White Radish

Ingredients:

White radish   some

Process and application:

Wash it clean, cut it into thick pieces, broil it over fire and before sleep lightly rub the affected part with it until the affected part becomes red. Apply it repeatedly until the frostbite is cured.

Curative properties: Frostbite (the affected part is red but does not fester).

White Pepper Powder

Ingredients:

White pepper   any amount

Process and application:

Grind the white pepper into fine powder, sift it through a fine sieve and preserve it in a bottle. Decoct some of unground white pepper in water and strain off the decoction. When the decoction becomes warm, bathe the affected part with it, wipe the affected part, apply the white pepper powder to the affected part and bandage it with absorbent cotton. Renew it once a day. It is necessary to apply this recipe 3 - 5 times to cure the ulcer.

Curative properties: Frostbite with ulcery.

Garlic Pulp

Ingredients:
Garlic (better purple-skin garlic)   any amount
Process and application:
Skin the garlic, cut it into pieces and pulp it. The treatment should begin from summer. Apply the pulp to the part where frostbite occured last winter. Wash it off the next day and resume applying it 3 or 4 days later.

Curative properties: Frostbite that occurs every year.

BURN; SCALD

Fresh Milk

Ingredients:
Fresh milk   some
Process and application:
Soak sterilized gauze in the milk and apply this gauze to the affected part.

Curative properties: Burn (The blister does not fester).

Hen's Egg White with White Spirit

Ingredients:
White spirit   15 ml
Hen's egg   1
Process and application:

Beat the egg and mix the egg white with the white spirit. Apply the mixture to the affected part.

Curative properties: Burn; scald.

Emulsion of Quick Lime and Unboiled Sesame Oil

Ingredients:

Quick lime	250 g
Unboiled sesame oil	250 ml

Process and application:

Put the quick lime in a clean basin and pour in 1000 ml water. When the quick lime breaks down, shake it for 5 - 10 minutes once in every 30 minutes. Repeat this 6 - 7 times. Leave it still for one day and one night and about 250 ml of the clear liquid from the surface is thus obtained. Mix the liquid and unboiled sesame oil into an emulsion. Apply this emulsion to the affected part 3 or 4 times a day. If the affected part has blistered, cut the blister with sterilized scissors before applying the emulsion.

Curative properties: Minor or medium burn with blisters or fester.

Potato Juice

Ingredients:

Potato	some

Process and application:

Peel the potato and wash it clean. Chop it, pound it into a mash and squeeze it in gauze to obtain the juice. Apply the juice to the affected part.

Curative properties: Minor burn.

Cucumber Juice

Ingredients:

Old cucumber   any amount

Process and application:

Cut the cucumber open, seed it, wrap it in gauze and squeeze its juice out. Sift the juice and preserve it in a bottle. Apply cotton balls soaked with the juice to the affected part.

Curative properties: Scald; burn; wound caused by wasp sting.

Pulp of Carrot

Ingredients:

Carrot   1

Process and application:

Wash the carrot and pulp it. Appy the pulp to the affected part.

Curative properties: Burn.

Leaves of Old Peking Cabbage

Ingredients:

Leaves of old Peking cabbage   5
Sesame oil   some

Process and application:

Roast the leaves until they become dry, pound them into fine powder and mix the powder with sesame oil into cream. Apply the cream to the affected part.

Curative properties: Scald, burn.

TRAUMATIC INJURY

Hen's Egg Shell Powder

Ingredients:

Hen's egg shell   some

Process and application:

Wash the egg-shell clean, roast it unitl it is dry and pound it into powder. Take 15 g powder at a time, twice a day.

Curative properties: Slow recovery of fracture.

Ointment from Rape-seed Oil, Shell of Freshwater Mussel and Egg-shell

Ingredients:

Shell of freshwater mussel   60 g
Hen's egg shell   60 g
Rape-seed oil   some

Process and application:

Roast the shell of freshwater mussel and egg-shell until they become charcoal, grind the charcoal into fine powder and mix the powder with rape-seed oil. Apply the ointment to the affected part.

Curative properties: Traumatic injury; abrasion.

Baked Loofah

Ingredients:

Old loofah (newly plucked)   1
White spirit   some

Process and application:

Cut the old loofah into slices and dry it in sun. Parch

it in an iron pan over slow fire until it becomes yellow-brown. Pound it into powder and preserve it in a bottle. The patient who suffers from traumatic injury in the breast or stomach takes an infusion of 3 g powder in white spirit at a time, twice a day, for 3 consecutive days; the patient who suffers in the limbs, mix the powder with white spirit and apply it to the affected part once a day.

Curative properties: Traumatic injury (with blood stasis and swelling).

Ointment of Chili Pepper

Ingredients:

Chili pepper	1 portion
Vaseline	5 portion

Process and application:

Grind the chili pepper into very fine powder. Melt the vaseline by heating. Mix them and stir them until the smell of chili pepper emits. Leave the mixture cool. Apply gauze and absorbent cotton with the ointment to the affected part. Renew it once every day or every other day.

Curative properties: Black swelling due to traumatic injury.

Powder of Shell of a Crab and Cucumber Seed

Ingredients:

Shell of a crab	1
Cucumber seed	15 g
Yellow rice or millet wine	some

Process and application:

Dry the shell of a crab and cucumber seed in sun and when dry, grind them into powder. Take an infusion of the powder in yellow rice or millet wine.

Curative properties: Traumatic injury (with blood stasis and swelling).

Chinese Flowering Crabapple Pulp

Ingredients:
Chinese flowering crabapple   250 g
Process and application:
Pulp the Chinese flowering crabapple and apply it to the affected part, once in every 13th hour.

Curative properties: Traumatic injury (with blood stasis and swelling).

Green Chinese Onion

Ingredients:
Green Chinese onion   some
Process and application:
Pulp the green Chinese onion and roast it until it becomes hot. Apply the hot pulp to the affected part and renew it when it becomes cold. Apply this consecutively several times.

Curative properties: Traumatic injury (with blooding).

BITE OR STING BY INSECTS, SNAKES OR ANIMALS

Soaked Tea Leaves

Ingredients:
Soaked tea leaves   some
Process and application:
Apply the tea leaves (soaked once and pounded) to the wound.

Curative properties: Sting of wasp or insects.

Tea

Ingredients:

Tea   6 g

Process and application:

Infuse the tea in hot water. Wash the wound with tea or apply it to the wound.

Curative properties: Sting by insects with local swelling and itching all over the body, vexation and thirst.

Warm White Spirit

Ingredients:

White spirit   50 g

Process and application:

Pour the white spirit in a cup and warm it. Apply the warm white spirit to the affected spot.

Curative properties: Sting of wasp (with swelling and itching).

Pear Leaf Decoction

Ingredients:

Pear leaves   2 handfuls

Process and application:

Wash the leaves(dry or fresh) clean and decoct them in water. Drink one big bowl of the decoction (the patient will sweat) and at the same time wash the wound with the decoction.

Curative properties: Snake bite.

Green Chinese Onion Pulp with Honey

Ingredients:

Honey   30 g
Green Chinese onion   2

Process and application:

Wash the green Chinese onion clean and pulp it, mix it with honey and appy the mixture to the wound.

Curative properties: Snake bite; insect bite.

Hen's Egg

Ingredients:

Hen's egg   1

Process and application:

Cut a hole in the egg and stick the egg to the wound.

Curative properties: Bite of snakes, scorpions or spiders.

Extract from Rotten Chinese Yam

Ingredients:

Rotten Chinese yam (better with secretion)   some

Process and application:

Pound the rotten Chinese yam and squeeze its extract out for application to the wound.

Curative properties: Scorpion sting.

Fresh Aubergine

Ingredients:

Aubergine   1

Process and application:

Cut the aubergine open and rub the wound with it. Alternatively, pulp it and mix it with some white sugar for external application.

Curative properties: Wasp sting; centipede bite.

Fresh Peach Leaf

Ingredients:

Fresh peach leaves   any amount

Process and application:

Wash the leaves clean, chew them into paste. For the patient whose wound has not festered, apply the leaves to the wound; for those whose wound has festered, apply the leaves around the wound and the wound must not be touched by the leaves. Renew the leaves once a day. The amount of leaves applied is determined by the size of the wound. Wash the wound with salt water before applying the leaves.

Curative properties: Dog bite.

Salt Solution

Ingredients:

Table salt   some

Process and application:

Dissolve the salt in a little hot water and soak aseptic cotton with the solution. Wash the wound several times with the aseptic cotton until a slight pain is felt.

Curative properties: Scorpion sting.

Recipes for Dermatological Diseases

PRORIASIS (PSORIASIS)

White Spirit with a Pallas-pit Viper

Ingredients:

Pallas-pit viper	1
Ginseng	15 g
White spirit	1000 ml

Process and application:

Put the pallas-pit viper into a container and kill it by drowning it in the white spirit. Add ginseng and leave it infuse in the liquid for 7 days. Take any amount of the liquid at any time.

Curative properties: Proriasis.

Hen's Eggs Soaked in Mature Vinegar

Ingredients:

Fresh hen's eggs	10
Mature vinegar	some

Process and application:

Let the eggs soak in mature vinegar for 7 - 10 days. Take out the eggs and shell them. Mix the egg yolk and egg white even and preserve it in a bottle. Wash the affected spot for 2 minutes with cotton balls soaked with the mixture of egg white and yolk, several times each day.

Curative properties: Proriasis; neurodermatitis.

Pulp of Chinese Chives and Garlic

Ingredients:

Chinese chives	50 g
Garlic	50 g

Process and application:

Pulp the Chinese chives and skinned garlic together and heat the pulp over fire. Rub the affected part with the pulp once or twice a day, for several consecutive days.

Curative properties: Proriasis; it is also effective to allergic dermatitis.

Powder of Hoof's Nail of a Cow

Ingredients:

Hoof's nail of a cow	30 g
Sesame oil	a little

Process and application:

Roast the hoof's nail of a cow in fire until it becomes charcoal. Pound it into fine powder and mix the powder and sesame oil. Apply the mixture to the affected area once a day, for 15 consecutive days.

Curative properties: Proriasis at any part of the body.

Water Chestnut with Mature Vinegar

Ingredients:

Fresh water chestnuts	10
Mature Vinegar	75 ml

Process and application:

Peel the water chestnuts and cut them into pieces. Decoct them in mature vinegar over slow fire for no less than 10 minutes until the mature vinegar dries. Pulp the water chestnuts. Apply a little of the pulp to the affected part and rub it with gauze. When the affected part turns red, apply more pulp and cover the affected part with a piece of clean paper and bandage it. Apply it once a day, for consecutive days until the disease is cured.

Curative properties: Proriasis.

Pomegranate Rind Juice

Ingredients:
Fresh pomegranate rind and alum   some for each
Process and application:
Squeeze the pomegranate rind with both hands to extract its juice. Apply the juice with alum to the affected part, several times each day.

Curative properties: Proriasis.

TINEA

Soup of Fat Pork with Kelp

Ingredients:

Kelp (shredded)	120 g
Fat pork	100 g

Process and application:
Cook the above ingredients in clear water without any seasoning until they are done. Eat the soup with its contents.

Curative properties: Tinea unguium.

Garlic Ointment

Ingredients:
Garlic   some
Process and application:

Skin the garlic and pulp it, mix it and sesame oil or vaseline into an ointment. Shave the hair of the patient and apply it to the affected part, once every day or every other day. (The affected part burns a bit after the ointment is applied).

Curative properties: Porrigo.

Vinegar

Ingredients:

Vinegar   some

Process and application:

Contain the vinegar in a plastic bag and let the affected hand soak in the vinegar for a night. The curative effect will be achieved after several applications of this.

Curative properties: Tinea unguium; tinea unguium.

Rice Vinegar

Ingredients:

Rice vinegar   30 ml

Process and application:

Heat the rice vinegar in an iron pot over fire until it boils. Wash the affected part with cotton balls soaked with the rice vinegar, any times a day.

Curative properties: Ringworm of scalp.

Tobacco Leaf Decoction

Ingredients:

Tobacco leaf   150 g

Process and application:

Decoct the tobacco leaf in water. Apply the decoction to the affected part 2 or 3 times each day.

Curative properties: Porrigo.

Potato Mash

Ingredients:

Potato   some

Process and application:

Peel the potato and pound it into a mash. Apply the mash to the affected part and cover it with a piece of oil paper and bandage it, 5 times a day.

Curative properties: Tinea capitis.

Apricot Kernel Decoction in Mature Vinegar

Ingredients:

Mature vinegar   250 ml
Apricot kernel   15 g

Process and application:

Pestle the apricot kernel and boil it in the mature vinegar. Apply the decoction hot with cotton balls soaked with it to the affected part, once a day, for 3 consecutive days as a course of treatment. Resume the application 3 days later.

Curative properties: Various types of tinea.

Pericarp of Walnut

Ingredients:

Pericarps of unripe walnuts   10

Process and application:

Scrape the outer layer of unripe green walnuts to remove the pericarps. Rub the affected area with the moist pericarps 3 - 5 times a day. A curative effect will be felt after 15 days of continuous application. Alternatively dry the pericarps and decoct them in water. Wash the affected part with the decoction. The same curative effect will be achieved.

Curative properties: All kinds of tinea.

URTICARIA

Decoction of Fresh Ginger with Vinegar

Ingredients:

Fresh ginger	30 g
Brown sugar	100 g
Vinegar	100 ml

Process and application:
Cut the fresh ginger into fine shreds and decoct it with vinegar and brown sugar in water. Strain off the liquid. Take one small cup of the decoction warm with boiled water, 3 times a day.

Curative properties: Urticaria due to food allergy.

Toad Decoction for External Administration

Ingredients:

Toads	3 - 4

Process and application:
Gut the toads and wash them clean. Stew them in an earthenware pot until they become very soft. Strain off the decoction through gauze. Apply the decoction to the affected area, 3 - 4 times a day.

Curative properties: Papular urticaria.

Chinese Chives for External Administration

Ingredients:

Chinese chives	1 handful

Process and application:

Heat the Chinese chives over fire and rub the affected part with it, several times a day.

Curative properties: Urticaria.

Rice Gruel with Chinese Chives

Ingredients:

Chinese chives	80 g
Rice	100 g
Cooking oil, table salt and fresh ginger	some for each

Process and application:

Prepare rice gruel, put in Chinese chives (cut into pieces) together with oil, salt and fresh ginger shreds and continue cooking the gruel for a moment.

Curative properties: Urticaria.

ECZEMATOSIS

Mung Bean Flour Mixed with Sesame Oil

Ingredients:

Mung bean flour and sesame oil	some for each

Process and application:

Parch the mung bean flour until it becomes yellow, leave it cool and mix it with sesame oil. Apply the mixture to the affected part.

Curative properties: Eczematosis with yellowish ooze.

Roasted Walnut Kernel

Ingredients:

Walnut kernel   some

Process and application:

Pound the walnut kernel and roast it until it becomes yellow and oozes oil. Pound it into paste for application to the affected part. It is helpful to use this recipe regularly.

Curative properties: Various types of dermatitis, eczematosis.

White Sugar Water

Ingredients:

White sugar   120 g

Process and application:

Dissolve the white sugar in 2000 g clear water and heat the water until it boils. Put the hot water in a basin and heat the affected part with steam from the hot water. When the water cools to a suitable temperature, wash the affected part with it, twice a day for 2 consecutive days.

Curative properties: Eczema of scrotum.

Ointment of Skin of Broad Bean and Sesame Oil

Ingredients:

Skin of broad bean and sesame oil   some for each

Process and application:

Remove the skin from the soaked broad bean and dry the skin in sun. When dry, roast it over fire until it becomes brown. Grind it into fine powder and sift the powder through a sieve. Mix the powder and sesame oil into an ointment for external application. Apply it once a day.

Curative properties: Eczematosis; this ointment is especially effective for the affected part in head, face and ears.

Mash of Vegetables

Ingredients:

Fresh Peking cabbage, cabbage and carrot	some for each
Honey and table salt	a little for each

Process and application:

The above ingredients are applied in 2 alternative ways: (1.) Wash the above vegetables clean, cut them into pieces and cook them in boiling water for about 15 minutes. Fish them out, pulp them and mix the mash with some salt. Feed this mash to the patient. (2.) Wash the vegetables clean, cut them into pieces, heat some water (1 bowl of water for 2 bowls of vegetable) until it boils and put in the vegetables, continue cooking them for 5 minutes. Take the soup with some honey.

Curative properties: Infantile eczema.

Tomato Leaves

Ingredients:

Fresh and tender tomato leaves	some
Table salt	some
Talcum powder	a little

Process and application:

Wash the tomato leaves clean, cut them into pieces, add salt and pound them into a mash. Decoct the mash and wash the affected spot with the hot decoction. After that, apply the talcum powder to the affected part.

Curative properties: Eczema of scrotum.

Olive Decoction

Ingredients:

Olive   100 g

Process and application:

Pound the olive and decoct it in 1000 g clear water over slow fire until half of the decoction is left. Strain off the liquid and wash the affected part with the decoction for half an hour, several times a day. The curative effect will be achieved after several days' application of this decoction.

Curative properties: Superficial ulcer of scrotum.

Centipede Powder Mixed with Pig's Bile

Ingredients:

Centipedes   3

Pig's bile   a little

Process and application:

Roast the centipedes until they become dry, grind them into powder and mix the power with pig's bile. Apply the mixture to the affected area.

Curative properties: Obstinate eczematosis.

Recipes for Gynecological Diseases

DYSMENORRHEA

Decoction of Dried Ginger, Chinese-date and Brown Sugar

Ingredients:

Dried ginger	30 g
Chinese-date	30 g
Brown sugar	30 g

Process and application:

Wash the Chinese-date and stone it. Wash the dried ginger and cut it into slices. Decoct the above along with brown sugar in water and take the decoction warm, twice a day.

Curative properties: Dysmenorrhea.

Decoction of Chinese Angelica Root

Ingredients:

Chinese angelica root	10 g

Process and application:

Cut the Chinese angelica root into pieces and decoct it in water. Take the decoction as a drink.

Curative properties: Dysmenorrhea.

Argyi Leaf Decoction with Brown Sugar

Ingredients:

| Argyi leaf | 20 g |
| Brown sugar | 15 g |

Process and application:
Decoct the above ingredients in water and take the decoction as a drink.

Curative properties: Dysmenorrhea.

Hen's Egg Boiled with Argyi Leaf and Fresh Ginger

Ingredients:

Argyi leaf	10 g
Fresh ginger	15 g
Hen's eggs	2

Process and application:
Boil the eggs in water with the other ingredients until the eggs are done. Take one dose each day, for 7 consecutive days.

Curative properties: Abdominal pain after menstruation.

Black Soya-bean and Hen's Eggs with Rice Wine

Ingredients:

Black soya-bean	60 g
Hen's eggs	2
Rice wine	120 ml

Process and application:
Cook the black soyabean and eggs until the eggs are done. Shell the eggs and continue cooking them until the black soyabean are done. Add rice wine and take the soup with black soyabean and eggs.

Curative properties: Dysmenorrhea; irregular menstruation.

Decoction of Hawthorn Fruit
and Sunflower Seed

Ingredients:

Hawthorn fruit	40 g
Sunflower seed	20 g
Brown sugar	30 g

Process and application:

Roast the hawthorn fruit and sunflower seeds (rid of the husk) together until they are done. Pound them and decoct them in water until the decoction becomes thick. Take the decoction with brown sugar, 2 or 3 times consecutively before menstruation.

Curative properties: Dysmenorrhea.

Hen's Eggs and Brown Sugar

Ingredients:

Hen's eggs	2
Brown sugar	100 g

Process and application:

Mix the brown sugar in a little water, heat the water until it boils and beat the eggs in it to prepare a half-done egg soup. Take it once a day, 2 or 3 times after the menstruation.

Curative properties: Dysmenorrhea; irregular menstruation.

Chinese Rose Decoction with Crystal Sugar

Ingredients:

Chinese roses	5
Crystal sugar	50 g

Process and application:
Decoct the flowers in 2 cups of water in a pot until 1 cup of decoction is left and add crystal sugar to it. Take the decoction hot, once a day, for 3 consecutive days as a course of treatment.

Curative properties: Dysmenorrhea.

MENORRHAGIA

Strong Tea with Brown Sugar

Ingredients:

Tea and brown sugar	some for each

Process and application:
Prepare a cup of strong tea and dissolve brown sugar in it. Take it twice a day.

Curative properties: Menorrhagia.

Decoction of Black Fungus and Chinese-date

Ingredients:

Black fungus	30 g
Chinese-dates	20

Process and application:
Decoct the above ingredients for drinking. Take the decoction once a day and take it continuously.

Curative properties: Anemia; menorrhagia; bleeding due to hemorrhoids.

Lotus Seed Decoction

Ingredients:

Tea	5 g
Lotus seed	30 g

Crystal sugar   20 g

Process and application:

Prepare tea in hot water and strain the dregs from the tea. Let the lotus seeds soak in warm water for several hours. Put in crystal sugar and stew the lotus seeds until they are very soft. Mix them with the tea for drinking.

Curative properties: Menorrhagia.

Oyster Soup

Ingredients:

Fresh oyster meat   250 g
Chicken soup and lean pork soup   some for each
Table salt and gourmet powder   a little for each

Process and application:

Heat the oyster meat, chicken soup and lean pork soup until boiling. Take the soup with its contents after seasoning it with salt and gourmet powder.

Curative properties: Menorrhagia.

METRORRHAGIA AND METROSTAXIS (DYSFUNCTIONAL UTERINE BLEEDING)

Silkworm Cocoon with Yellow Rice or Millet Wine

Ingredients:

Silkworm cocoon   3 g
Yellow rice or millet wine   some

Process and application:

Pound the silkworm cocoons into fine powder and take an infusion of the powder in warm yellow rice or millet wine.

Curative properties: Persistent endometrorrhagia.

146

Sophora Flower with Rice Wine

Ingredients:

Sophora flower	15 g
Rice wine	a little

Process and application:

Broil the sophora flower until it becomes brown, pound it into fine powder and take an infusion of it in rice wine.

Curative properties: Persistent endometrorrhagia.

Cotton-seed Cake Powder with Yellow Rice or Millet Wine

Ingredients:

Cotton-seed cake	60 - 120 g
Yellow rice or millet wine	some

Process and application:

Parch the cotton-seed cake in an earthenware pot until it becomes dry (but not burnt), grind it into fine powder and take an infusion of the powder in yellow rice or millet wine.

Curative properties: Dysfunctional uterine bleeding.

Black Fungus Gruel

Ingredients:

Black fungus (or white jellyfungus)	5 g
Chinese-dates	5
Rice	100 g
Crystal sugar	some

Process and application:

Soften the black fungus(or white jellyfungus) by soaking it in warm water and rid it of the impurities and the stems. Tear it up, cook it with washed rice and Chinese-dates in water over strong fire until boiling. Continue heating them over slow fire until they become very soft gruel. Dissolve crystal sugar in the gruel. It should be avoided by pregnant women and those who suffer from fever due to cold.

Curative properties: Dysfunctional uterine bleeding; bleeding due to hemorrhoids.

Cotton Hibiscus Flower Decoction

Ingredients:

Cotton hibiscus flower	30 g

Process and application:

Decoct it in water and take one decoction in 2 or 3 separate portions every day until the bleeding is arrested.

Curative properties: Dysfunctional uterine bleeding.

Hen Stewed with Argyi Leaf

Ingredients:

Old argyi leaf	30 g
Old hen (preferably, black bone hen)	1
Yellow rice or millet wine	50 g
Table salt	some

Process and application:

Kill the hen, deplume it, gut it and wash it clean. Wash the argyi leaf clean and wrap it in clean gauze. Put the hen and argyi leaf with yellow rice or millet wine in water in an earthenware pot to cook until the chicken is very soft. Add salt to the soup. Eat all the soup with chicken in one day. If the endometrorrhagia is not arrested, resume taking this soup 3 - 5 days later. Raw or cold food should be avoided.

Curative properties: Colporrhagia.

Cooked Black Fungus with Brown Sugar

Ingredients:

Black fungus	30 g
Brown sugar	20 g

Process and application:

Cook the black fungus in water over slow fire and when done, add the brown sugar. Take this in 2 separate doses in one day.

Curative properties: Endometrorrhagia.

Jelly of Carp Scale and Yellow Rice or Millet Wine

Ingredients:

Carp scale	200 g
Yellow rice or millet wine	some

Process and application:

Wash the carp scales clean and boil them in water over slow fire to make jelly. Take an infusion of all the jelly in 60 g of warm yellow rice or millet wine, in 2 separate doses in one day.

Curative properties: Endometrorrhagia.

Steamed Black-bone Chicken

Ingredients:

Black-bone chicken	1
Argyi leaf	20 g
Yellow rice or millet wine	30 ml

Process and application:

Deplume, gut and bleed the black-bone chicken, add argyi leaf, yellow rice or millet wine and a cup of water to it and steam it until it is done and very soft. Eat the soup and the chicken after seasoning it with a little table salt and take it with bread or cooked rice.

Curative properties: Endometrorrhagia.

MORBID LEUKORRHEA
(PELVIC INFLAMMATION ; CERVICITIS)

Pomegranate Rind Decoction

Ingredients:

Pomegranate rind	30 g

Process and application:

Decoct it in water and take the decoction as a drink.

Curative properties: Leukorrhea; soreness of waist and abdominal pain.

Cockcomb Flower with Fresh Lotus Root Juice

Ingredients:

Fresh cockcomb flower	500 g
Fresh lotus root juice	500 ml
White sugar	500 g

Process and application:

Wash the cockcomb flower clean and decoct it in water. Strain off the liquid once every 20 minutes and add water to continue decocting it until 3 decoctions have been extracted. Combine the 3 decoctions together and boil this over slow fire until thick soup is obtained. Then put in the fresh lotus root juice and heat the soup until it becomes thick and sticky. Move it from the fire and put in white sugar to absorb the decoction. Dry it in sun and when dry,

150

grind it into powder and preserve the powder in a bottle for later use. Take an infusion of 10 g powder in hot water in 3 separate doses each day.

Curative properties: Morbid leukorrhea; Trichomonas vaginalis; vaginitis.

Patty of Hen's Egg and Pepper

Ingredients:

Pepper	27 pcs
Hen's egg	1

Process and application:

Grind the pepper into fine powder, beat the egg and mix it with the powder. Fry the mixture until it becomes a patty. Take the patty for breakfast, consecutively for half a month.

Curative properties: Watery leukorrhea.

Cactus for Internal and External Administration

Ingredients:

Cactus (flesh of the tuber and the fruit)	80 g
Cactus (whole plant)	100 g
Lean pork	60 - 90 g
Table salt	a little

Process and application:

Wash the tuber of cactus and the pork clean and chop them. Put them in an earthenware bowl and season them with flavorings. Heat them by putting the bowl in boiling water until they are very soft. Take the soup 2 or 3 times a day. At the same time wash the whole plant of cactus clean, chop it and add a little table salt. Put it in a basin to boil for 15 minutes. Steam and wash the vulva with this hot decoction once every night. Use the cactus for internal and external administration simultaneously for 10 consecutive days as a course of treatment. If the disease is not cured, take another course. The treatment should be ceased temporarily during menstrual onset.

Curative properties: Leukorrhea with reddish discharge with pruritus of vulva and soreness of waist.

Lotus Seed Pill

Ingredients:

Lotus seed	200 g
Buckwheat flour	200 g
Hen's eggs	6

Process and application:

Pestle the lotus seeds into powder, beat the eggs and mix the powder with the egg white and buckwheat flour to roll pills in size to a mung bean. Take 10 g of the pill before meal with warm water each day.

Curative properties: Excessive leukorrhea; general asthenia; soreness of waist and debility of lumbus.

Soup of Cowpea and Chicken

Ingredients:

Cowpea	150 g
Chicken	100 g
Table salt, prickly-ash peel, gourmet powder	some of each

Process and application:

Wash the cowpea clean, rid it of the stems and strings and cut it into short sections. Stew it with chicken and prickly-ash peel for 1 hour. Add some salt and gourmet powder to the soup and take it with bread or cooked rice. It is helpful to use this recipe regularly.

Curative properties: Morbid leukorrhea.

Gruel with Lotus Seed and Dried Longan Pulp

Ingredients:

Lotus seed	20 g
Dried longan pulp	30 g
Glutinous rice	60 g
Chinese-dates	9
White sugar	50 g

Process and application:

Cook the above ingredients in water until they become gruel. Take the gruel once a day, for 10 consecutive days as a course of treatment.

Curative properties: Morbid leukorrhea.

HYPEREMESIS GRAVIDARUM

Drink of Sugarcane and Fresh Ginger

Ingredients:

Sugarcane juice	10 g
Fresh ginger juice	10 g

Process and application:

Mix the above juices and sip a bit of the juice at short intervals.

Curative properties: Hyperemesis gravidarum.

Glutinous Rice Soup

Ingredients:

Glutinous rice	30 g (for 1 dose)

Process and application:

Cook glutinous rice soup and take it 4 times a day.

Hard and cold food should be avoided.

Curative properties: Vomiting after 2 months of pregnancy and medicine produces no effect.

Chinese Chives and Fresh Ginger Extract

Ingredients:

Chinese chives	200 g
Fresh ginger	200 g
White sugar	some

Process and application:

Cut Chinese chives and fresh ginger into pieces and pound them to obtain the extract. Take the extract after mixing it with sugar.

Curative properties: Hyperemesis gravidarum with syndrome of anorexia.

Decoction of Shaddock Ped, Fresh Ginger and Chinese-date

Ingredients:

Shaddock ped (preferably, old one)	1
Fresh ginger	3 - 5 slices
Chinese-dates	5 - 7

Process and application:

Wash the above ingredients clean, cut the shaddock ped into small pieces and decoct it in 500 ml of water until 300 ml decoction is left. Then add fresh ginger and Chinese-dates and continue decocting them over slow fire for 30 minutes. Strain off the liquid and take it at any time. Alternatively, take the liquid after mixing it with some white sugar.

Curative properties: Hyperemesis gravidarum.

154

Lemon Preserved In Granulated Sugar

Ingredients:

Lemon (fresh)	500 g
White granulated sugar	250 g

Process and application:

Wash the lemon clean and soak it in warm water for one hour. Peel it, stone it and cut it into long narrow pieces. Put the lemon into a basin, add 100 g of the granulated sugar and mix them well. Cover the basin and let the lemon soak in sugar for one day and one night. After this, take out the lemon and heat it in water over fire until it boils. Continue heating it over slow fire until the decoction is dry. Then put in the remaining sugar (dissolved in a little water) and continue stewing it over slow fire until the lemon absorbs all sugar. Move it from the fire and leave it to cool off. Keep it in a dry place. Take the lemon at any time, sucking it in the mouth, swallowing down the saliva secreted and chewing the lemon.

Curative properties: Hyperemesis gravidarum.

Grape Juice

Ingredients:

Fresh grape	1000 g
White sugar	100 g

Process and application:

Wash the grapes clean, pound them, sieve them through a sieve and strain off the extract. Put some sugar in the juice and take 50 - 100 g of it at a time, twice a day.

Curative properties: Hyperemesis gravidarum.

155

Olive Decoction

Ingredients:

Olive   any amount

Process and application:

Wash the olive clean, pulp it and decoct it. Take the decoction 2 or 3 times a day.

Curative properties: Hyperemesis gravidarum.

Decoction of Radish Seed, Fresh Ginger and Shaddock Ped

Ingredients:

Radish seed	15 g
Fresh ginger	15 g
Shaddock ped	15 g

Process and application:

Decoct the above ingredients in one bowlful of water in a pot until half a bowl of decoction is left.

Curative properties: Hyperemesis gravidarum.

THREATENED ABORTION
(THREATENED ABORTION; HABITUAL ABORTION)

Lotus Seed and Raisin

Ingredients:

Lotus seed	90 g
Raisin	30 g

Process and application:

Peel and seed the lotus seeds, wash them clean and put them with raisin in an earthenware pot. Add 700 - 800 ml of water in the pot and heat them by putting the pot in

156

boiling water over strong fire until the lotus seeds are very soft and done. Take them once a day and it will exert effect after taking it 5 to 10 times.

Curative properties: Threatened abortion.

Decoction of Walnut

Ingredients:

Walnuts   10

Process and application:

Crack the walnuts and decoct them with the shells in water. Strain the decoction and take it as a drink.

Curative properties: Threatened abortion.

Steamed Egg Yolk with Yellow Rice or Millet Wine

Ingredients:

Yolk (of hen's eggs)   5
Yellow rice or millet wine   50 ml

Process and application:

Mix the ingredients well. Add some water and table salt and steam them for one hour. Take it at a draft or in separate doses.

Curative properties: Threatened abortion.

Gruel with Black Soyabean and Glutinous Rice

Ingredients:

Black soyabean   30 g
Glutinous rice   60 g

Process and application:

Wash the above ingredients clean, put them in a pot and cook them in water over slow fire until they become gruel. Take the gruel at a draft or in separate doses.

Curative properties: Threatened abortion.

Soup of Ramie and Hen's Egg

Ingredients:

Ramie	50 g
Hen's eggs	4

Process and application:

Wash the ramie in cold water, remove the gummy substance by bathing it in hot water, put it in a pot and boil it in water. Beat the eggs in the pot and continue heating the soup for half an hour. Take the soup with the contents.

Curative properties: Abdominal pain and lumbago due to threatened abortion.

Cooked Chinese-date and Sweet Potato

Ingredients:

Sweet potato	30 g
Chinese-dates	10

Process and application:

Cut the sweet potato into cubes, cook it with Chinese-dates in water until they are done. Add one spoonful of brown sugar.

Curative properties: Threatened abortion.

Soup of Chinese-date and Hen's Eggs

Ingredients:

Chinese-dates	5
Hen's eggs	2

Process and application:

Cook the Chinese-dates in water until they are nearly

158

done, beat the eggs in it and heat the soup until the eggs are done. Take the eggs with the liquid once a day.

Curative properties: Threatened abortion.

Soup of Argyi Leaf and Hen's Egg

Ingredients:

Fresh argyi leaf	15 g
Hen's egg	1

Process and application:

Decoct the argyi leaf in water to get a thick soup and beat the egg in the soup. Take the soup once a day on an empty stomach, and take it consecutively for a month.

Curative properties: Habitual abortion.

Steamed Glutinous Rice Flour with Hen's Eggs

Ingredients:

Glutinous rice flour	40 g
Hen's eggs	2

Process and application:

Beat the eggs, mix them with the glutinous rice flour and steam them until they are done. Take this recipe at a draft, once a day. Take it several times consecutively if necessary.

Curative properties: Threatened abortion with syndrome of abdominal pain.

Syrup of Sesame Oil and Honey

Ingredients:

Sesame oil	100 g
Honey	200 g

Process and application:

Heat the above ingredients over slow fire separately until they boils, leave them cool off and then mix them well. Take one spoonful of the syrup at a time, twice a day.

Curative properties: Threatened abortion.

Gruel with Carp and Ass-hide Glue

Ingredients:

Carp	1 (weight about 500 g)
Ass-hide glue	30 g
Glutinous rice	100 g

Process and application:

Descale and gut the carp, wash it clean and cut it into cakes. Cook it with glutinous rice in water until they become gruel. Add ass-hide glue, green Chinese onion, fresh ginger, table salt and continue boiling the gruel for 10 minutes. Take the gruel for lunch, once a day, consecutively for a week.

Curative properties: Miscarriage prevention and hemostasis.

HYPOGALACTIA

Dried, Shelled Shrimps with Yellow Rice or Millet Wine

Ingredients:

Dried, shelled shrimps	1000 g
Yellow rice or millet wine	1000 ml

Process and application:

Crush the dried, shelled shrimps and mix 2 spoonfuls of it with one cup of yellow rice or millet wine. Take the mixture warm, 3 times a day.

Curative properties: Galactostasis.

Cucumber Stewed in Liquor

Ingredients:
Cucumber and liquor   some for each
Process and application:
Cook the cucumber in some liquor until the cucumber is soft. Take the liquor and swallow the cucumber after chewing it. This recipe exerts curative effect promptly.

Curative properties: Galactostasis.

Sweet Potato Gruel

Ingredients:
Sweet potato   200 g
Rice   100 g
Process and application:
Skin the sweet potato, cut it into cakes, wash the rice clean and cook them in water until they become gruel. It should be avoided by those who suffer from diabetes, gastric ulcer or hyperhydrochloria.

Curative properties: Galactostasis.

Gruel with Carp Extract

Ingredients:
Carp   1 (weight about 500 g)
Rice   100 g
Fresh ginger dust   a little
Green Chinese onions   2
Sesame oil   a little
Cooking wine   several drops

| Table salt | very little |

Process and application:

Cut the live carp open, gut it but do not descale it, wash it clean and cook it in water over slow fire. Put in the fresh ginger dust and cooking wine and continue cooking it until the bones are loose. Remove the bones from the broth. Cook gruel with the rice, when the gruel becomes thick, mix it with the broth and salt well. Then continue heating the gruel for a moment. Take the gruel after adding sesame oil and green Chinese onion, in the morning and in the evening on an empty stomach.

Curative properties: Lack of milk secretion after childbirth.

Pig's Trotters with Yellow Rice or Millet Wine

Ingredients:

| Pig's trotter | 1 |
| Yellow rice or millet wine | 60 ml |

Process and application:

Cut the pig's trotter in halves, add some water and cook it over strong fire until the pig's trotter is overdone. Take it after adding yellow rice or millet wine.

Curative properties: Galactostasis.

Soup of Pig's Trotters with Peanut Kernels and Soy Bean

Ingredients:

Peanut kernels	60 g
Soy bean	60 g
Pig's trotters	2

Process and application:

Stew the pig's trotters for half an hour, remove the

162

foam, put in the peanut kernels and soy bean and continue heating them until the pig's trotters are done and soft. Eat the pig's trotters and/or eat the soup, twice a day.

Curative properties: Lack of milk secretion after childbirth.

Soup of Pig's Fore Trotters with Black Sesame Seed

Ingredients:

Pig's fore trotter	1
Black sesame seed	25 g

Process and application:

Cook soup with a pig's fore trotter over slow fire. Roast the sesame seeds until they become brown. Pound them into fine powder. Take an infusion of the sesame seed powder in the soup 3 times a day.

Curative properties: Lack of milk secretion after childbirth.

Broth of Knuckle of a Pig and Ham

Ingredients:

Knuckle of a pig (rid of big bones) and Ham	some for each

Process and application:

Stew the above ingredients in clear water with a little salt and take the broth after seasoning it with Jew's ear and "fragrant mushroom"(*Lentinus edodes*).

Curative properties: Thin and scanty secretion of milk after childbirth.

Hairtail Soup

Ingredients:

Hairtail   200 g

Process and application:

Rid the hairtail of the head, gills and entrails, wash it clean and cut it into sections. Cook it in water until it becomes very soft. Take the soup with the hairtail 3 times a day.

Curative properties: Galactostasis or deficient milk secretion.

Red Phaseolus Bean Gruel

Ingredients:

Red phaseolus bean   some

Process and application:

Cook red phaseolus bean gruel in water in the way as the ordinary gruel is cooked.

Curative properties: Galactostasis after childbirth.

Recipes for Children's Diseases

PERTUSSIS

Decoction of Loquat Leaf and Peach Kernel

Ingredients:

Loquat leaf	9 g
Peach kernel	5 pcs

Process and application:

Remove the hair from the loquat leaf and decoct the above ingredients in water. Take the decoction as a drink.

Curative properties: Paroxysmal spasmodic cough of pertussis with syndromes of abundant expectoration and vomiting.

Salted Kumquat Infused in Sugar Water

Ingredients:

Ripe kumquat, table salt and sugar   some for each

Process and application:

Pluck the ripe kumquat and preserve them in salt in a glass container for half a year. Take 2 - 4 kumquats and wash them with clear water, pulp them, dissolve the pulp in hot sugar water and strain the dregs from the liquid. Take this liquid twice a day.

Curative properties: Pertussis.

Duck's Egg Custard with Crystal Sugar

Ingredients:

Duck's egg	1
Crystal sugar	50 g

Process and application:

Dissolve crystal sugar in a cup of hot water and beat the duck's egg in it. Steam it until it becomes custard. Take the custard once in the morning on an empty stomach. For serious case another dose before sleep at night is necessary.

Curative properties: Restoration stage of pertussis with syndrome of frequent cough with dyspnea.

Decoction of Mung Bean and Olive

Ingredients:

Olives	5
Mung bean	500 g
White sugar	50 g

Process and application:

Decoct olives and mung bean in water and add sugar to it. Take the decoction with mung bean, once a day, for 5 consecutive days as a course of treatment.

Curative properties: Pertussis.

Gruel with Red-skin Radish[*] and Chinese-date

Ingredients:

Red-skin radish	150 g
Chinese-dates	12

---

[*] Red-skin radish is a var. of *Raphanus sativus* with red skin and white flesh.

| Rice | 100 g |
| White sugar | some |

Process and application:

Cut the red-skin radish into slices and cook it with rice and Chinese-dates in water. Season it with sugar. Take this gruel for breakfast or supper, once a day, for 10 consecutive days as course of treatment.

Curative properties: Pertussis.

Garlic Infusion

Ingredients:

| Garlic | 60 g |
| White sugar | some |

Process and application:

Skin the garlic and chop it, let it soak in 300 ml of cold boiled water for 10 hours. Strain the liquid and take it with a little sugar. Dosage for children older than 5 years is 15 ml, for younger children, half the dosage. Take it once in every other hour.

Curative properties: Pertussis.

Peanut Kernels and Crystal Sugar

Ingredients:

| Crystal sugar | 500 g |
| Peanut kernels | 250 g |

Process and application:

Heat the crystal sugar in a little water in a pot over slow fire until it has melted(in such a state that if you dip the slice in it and take the slice out, thin threads drip from the slice, but it does not stick to the hand), remove it from the fire and put in roasted peanut kernels when the crystal sugar is still hot. Mix them well and pour them in a big mug coated with cooking oil, press them, cool them off and cut them into small cakes before eating. This recipe can be taken regularly.

Curative properties: Pertussis.

Syrup of Walnut Kernel and Pear

Ingredients:

Walnut kernel	30 g
Crystal sugar	30 g
Pears	150 g

Process and application:
Wash the pears clean and decore them. Pound them with walnut kernel and crystal sugar, cook them in water until they become thick syrup. Take one spoonful of the syrup at time, 3 times a day.

Curative properties: Pertussis.

MEASLES

Paste of Buckwheat Flour and Egg White (for External Administration)

Ingredients:

Egg white and buckwheat flour	some for each
Sesame oil	several drops

Process and application:
Mix the above ingredients into paste and rub the breast, back and limbs of the suffering child with this paste.

Curative properties: Measles without adequate eruption.

Decoction of Water Chestnut and Sugarcane

Ingredients:

Water chestnut	250 g
Sugarcane	500 g
Red-skin radish*	

Process and application:

Wash the water chestnut clean. Split the sugarcane and cut it into sections. Wash the red-skin radish clean and cut it into cakes. Decoct the above in water for one hour and leave it cool. Take the decoction.

Curative properties: Persistent low fever after eruption of measles.

Soup of Crucian Carp and Mushroom

Ingredients:

Fresh mushroom	20 g
Crucian carp (live)	1 (in weight 250 g)

Process and application:

Cut the crucian carp open, descale it and gut it. Wash the mushroom clean. Put the above into an earthenware pot and add a little salt and one bowl of water, heat the water until it boils. Continue stewing it over slow fire until the crucian carp is very soft. Eat all the crucian carp with the soup in one day. Stop taking this recipe upon eruption of measles.

Curative properties: Insufficient eruption of measles.

---

* Red-skin radish is a var. of *Raphanus sativus* with red skin and white flesh.

Decoction of Fresh Water Chestnut

Ingredients:

Fresh water chestnuts	10
Juice of fresh radish	500 ml
Crystal sugar	a little

Process and application:

Peel the water chestnuts and wash them clean, add 500 ml of water and decoct them until 300 ml of decoction is left. Strain the water chestnuts from the liquid and dissolve the crystal sugar in the hot decoction. Mix this well with the radish juice after it cools off. Drink 100 ml of the decoction warm at a time, twice a day.

Curative properties: Residual heat, persistent dry cough after eruption of measles.

Soup of Bamboo Shoot and Crucian Carp

Ingredients:

Bamboo shoot	1
Crucian carp	1

Process and application:

Peel the bamboo shoot and cut it into pieces. Gut (but do not descale) the crucian carp. Stew the above until they are done. Take the soup.

Curative properties: Measles.

Decoction of Carrot and Coriander

Ingredients:

Carrot	120 g
Coriander	100 g
Water chestnut	60 g

Process and application:
Wash them clean and decoct them in water. Take the decoction as a drink.

Curative properties: Measles.

Cooked Pigeon Egg

Ingredients:

Pigeon eggs   2

Process and application:
Put the pigeon eggs in cold water in a pot and cook them. Remove the shells when the pigeon eggs are done. Take 2 pigeon eggs each day.

Curative properties: This recipe is effective in preventing children from catching measles when this is epidemic.

DIARRHEA IN CHILDREN

Decoction of Roasted Rice

Ingredients:

Rice   50 g

Process and application:
Parch the rice in a pan until it becomes black. Decoct it in one cup of water. Take the decoction.

Curative properties: Vomiting of milk in children.

Mung Bean and Pepper (for External Administration)

Ingredients:

Mung beans   3
Pepper   3 pcs
Chinese-dates   2

Process and application:

Wash the Chinese-dates clean and stone them, pound them together with mung beans and pepper and apply this mixture to the navel.

Curative properties: Dysentery with bloody stool, dysentery with mucus or purulent discharge in children.

Apple Mash

Ingredients:

Apple   1

Process and application:

Wash the apple clean, peel it, cut it into slices, put it in a bowl and cover the bowl. Steam it and pound it into a mash. Feed the mash to the suffering child.

Curative properties: Diarrhea in children with syndromes of thirst and anorexia.

Paste of Mung Bean Flour and Egg White

Ingredients:

Mung bean flour   9 g
Hen's egg white   1

Process and application:

Mix the above ingredients into paste. Apply this paste to the forehead of the vomiting child or to the sole to the child suffering from diarrhea.

Curative properties: Persistent vomiting, diarrhea in children in summer.

Paste of Hawthorn Fruit and Chinese Yam

Ingredients:

Hawthorn fruit, Chinese yam and
   white sugar   some for each

Process and application:
Wash the hawthorn fruit(stoned), Chinese yam clean and steam them. Add sugar to them and press them into paste after they cool off.

Curative properties: Diarrhea in children.

Chestnut Jam with White Sugar

Ingredients:

Chestnuts	10
White sugar	25 g

Process and application:
Peel the chestnuts, cook them into jam and season the jam with sugar. Take the jam twice a day.

Curative properties: Diarrhea in children.

Lotus Root Starch Soup

Ingredients:

Lotus root starch	30 g

Process and application:
Boil it in 120 ml of water until 100 ml decoction is left. Take the decoction in 3 separate doses in one day. (If the infant suffers serious diarrhea, treat it with medicine under the doctor's direction.)

Curative properties: Diarrhea for infant up to half a year old.

Pepper Powder Pastry

Ingredients:

Pepper powder	1 g
Cooked rice	15 g

Process and application:

Make a small pastry from newly steamed rice by pressing the latter with palms, scatter the pepper powder to its center. When it cools off, apply this pastry to the navel and bandage it. Remove the pastry after 4 - 8 hours. In case of serious dehydration, apply fluid infusion at the same time when this paste is applied.

Curative properties: Diarrhea in children.

MALDIGESTION IN CHILDREN

Carrot Decoction

Ingredients:

Carrot   250 g

Process and application:

Decoct the carrot in water and add a bit brown sugar. Take this as a drink at short intervals.

Curative properties: Retention of food; abdominal distension; persisting vomiting and diarrhea; incessant crying in children.

Pear Gruel

Ingredients:

Pears	3
Rice	100 g
Crystal sugar	some

Process and application:

Wash the pear clean, chop it and pound it to extract its juice. Wash the rice clean and cook it in water over strong fire until it boils, move it over to slow fire and continue cooking the gruel for half an hour. Add the pear juice to the gruel and take a little of it at a time, 2 or 3 times a day. This recipe should be avoided by those who have loose stools.

Curative properties: Infantile indigestion with syndrome of food retention and anorexia.

Gruel of Tripe from a Cow

Ingredients:

Tripe from a cow	150 - 200 g
Rice	40 - 50 g

Process and application:
Rub the tripe from a cow with table salt and rinse it clean. Cut it up, cook it along with rice and some clear water until they become gruel. Take the gruel after seasoning it with flavorings.

Curative properties: Infantile indigestion with food retention; anorexia.

Gruel with Quail

Ingredients:

Quail	1
Rice	some

Process and application:
Deplume and gut the quail, wash it clean, cut it into cubes and cook it with rice to prepare gruel. Take the gruel with flavorings.

Curative properties: Infantile indigestion with food retention; anorexia.

Cooked Rice with Frog

Ingredients:

Frogs	5 - 8
Peanut oil,	a little

175

| Table salt | a little |
| Rice | 100 g |

Process and application:

Skin the frogs, gut them, wash them clean, cut them into cubes and mix them with peanut oil and salt. Cook the rice in water, when the pot boils, put in the frogs and continue cooking the rice in covered pot over slow fire until the rice and frogs are done.

Curative properties: Infantile indigestion with the syndrome of food retention and ochriasis and emaciation.

Fried Silkworm Chrysalis

Ingredients:

Silkworm chrysalis	100 g
Cooking oil	some
Table salt	some

Process and application:

Heat cooking oil in a pot over fire, when the oil is hot, put in silkworm chrysalises and stir-fry them until they become bright yellow. Season them with salt before taking.

Curative properties: Infantile indigestion with food retention; leanness.

Apple Juice with Milk

Ingredients:

Apple juice (extracted from	
apple by pressing it)	70 g
White sugar	30 g
Milk	150 g

Process and application:

Dissolve the sugar in the apple juice, pour in hot boil-

176

ing milk and mix them well. Take the liquid warm once a day, for 10 consecutive days as a course of treatment.

Curative properties: Anorexia; lassitude.

RICKETS IN CHILDREN

Powder of Hen's Egg Shell

Ingredients:

Hen's egg shell   some

Process and application:

Wash the egg-shell clean, dry it over fire and grind it into fine powder. Children under the age of 1 year take 0. 5 g of the powder at a time and children of the age of 1 - 2 years take 1 g at a time, twice a day.

Curative properties: Rickets in children; tenany.

Broth of Bone from the Carcass of a Pig with Spinach

Ingredients:

Spine of a pig or leg bone of a pig   some
Spinach   some

Process and application:

Smash the bones and boil them in water to obtain thick broth, put in the spinach (washed clean and cut into short sections) and continue cooking them for a short while. Eat the broth with the spinach and the bone marrow twice a day. This recipe can be taken continually.

Curative properties: Rickets in children.

Boiled River Snail

Ingredients:

River snail, soy sauce and vinegar   some for each
Process and application:
Wash the river snail clean, boil them in hot water until they are done. Pick out the meat and eat it with flavorings. This recipe can be taken often.

Curative properties: Infantile chondropathy due to disturbance of calcium metabolism.

Chinese Chestnut Pastry

Ingredients:

Chinese chestnut (uncooked)	500 g
White sugar	250 g

Process and application:
Cook the Chinese chestnut in water for half an hour, cool it off and peel it. Put it in a bowl and steam it for 40 minutes. Pulp the Chinese chestnut while it is hot, mix it with sugar and make pastry by pressing the pulp in a bottle cap. It is to be taken by the suffering children regularly.

Curative properties: Flaccidity of extremities in children; weakness.

Carrot Gruel

Ingredients:

Carrot	150 - 250 g
Rice	100 g

Process and application:
Wash the fresh carrot clean, chop it and cook it along with rice in water. Take the gruel warm. Flavorings like table salt, sugar, mutton, pork etc. can be added in accordance with personal taste.

Curative properties: Infantile chondropathy.

BED-WETTING IN CHILDREN

Decoction of Chinese Chives Root

Ingredients:

Chinese chives root 25 g

Process and application:

Wash the Chinese chives root clean, wrap it in gauze and squeeze it to extract the juice. Take the juice warm twice a day, for 10 consecutive days.

Curative properties: Bed-wetting in children.

Hen's Eggs Boiled with Tea

Ingredients:

Tea	8 g
Table salt	3 g
Hen's eggs	10

Process and application:

Boil the eggs and tea in a pot for 8 minutes, crack the egg-shells, put salt in the pot and continue cooking the eggs for 10 - 15 minutes. When eaten, dip the eggs in soy sauce. Take one egg at a time, twice a day.

Curative properties: Bed-wetting in children.

Gruel With Mullet

Ingredients:

Mullet	1 (weight 250 - 300 g)
Rice	some

Process and application:

Descale the mullet, gut it and head it, cook it with rice in water until they become gruel. Take the gruel with seasoning. Care must be taken not to be choked by the fish bone.

Curative properties: Bed-wetting in children.

Bulbs of Green Chinese Onion and Sulfur (for External Application)

Ingredients:

Bulbs of green Chinese onion	7 - 8
Sulfur	50 g

Process and application:

Pound the above into jet and apply the jet to the navel before sleep. Apply this recipe for 3 consecutive nights.

Curative properties: Bed-wetting in children.

Steamed Pastries with Chinese Chive Seeds

Ingredients:

Chinese chive seed and wheat flour   some for each

Process and application:

Pound the Chinese chive seeds into fine powder, mix the powder with a little flour, knead the dough to make pastries and steam them for eating.

Curative properties: Bed-wetting in children.

Hen's Egg with White Pepper

Ingredients:

White pepper	6 pcs
Hen's egg	1

Process and application:

Pound the white pepper into fine powder, cut a small hole in the egg-shell and insert the white pepper into the egg. Cover the hole with a piece of moist paper and steam the egg. Remove the shell and take the egg with bread or cooked rice in lunch, once a day, for 7 consecutive days.

Curative properties: Bed-wetting in children.

Walnut Kernel Gruel

Ingredients:

Walnut kernel	50 g
Rice	25 g
White sugar	25 g

Process and application:

Pestle the walnut kernel, cook it with rice in water and when done, add sugar to it. Take the gruel for supper or take it as a snack, once a day for 7- 20 consecutive days as a course of treatment. This gruel can be taken regularly. It should be avoided by those who have loose stools.

Curative proprties: Minimal brain dysfunction; bed-wetting in children.

Recipes for E. N. T. Diseases and Ophthalmological Diseases

OPHTHALMOLOGICAL DISEASES

Dragon Well Tea with Chrysanthemum Flower

Ingredients:

Chrysanthemum flower	10 g
Dragon Well tea	3 g

Process and application:

Infuse the above in hot water and take the infusion as a drink.

Curative properties: Acute conjunctivitis; photophobia.

Infusion of Wolfberry Fruit and White Chrysanthemum Flower

Ingredients:

Wolfberry fruit	10 g
White chrysanthemum flower	10 g

Process and application:

Infuse the above in hot water and take the infusion as a drink.

Curative properties: Diminution of vision; dizziness; night blindness.

Wolfberry Fruit and Pig Liver Soaked in White Spirit

Ingredients:

Wolfberry fruit	80 g
White spirit	250 ml
Pig liver	some

Process and application:

Pound the wolfberry fruit, put it in a clean bottle with white spirit, hermetically seal the bottle and let the wolfberry soak in the white spirit for 7 days. Cook the pig liver and cut it into pieces. Take the pig liver (seasoned with salt and prickly-ash peel) along with the wolfberry fruit and 25 - 50 ml of the white spirit.

Curative properties: Vague sight; lacrimation induced by irritation of the wind.

Sheep Liver Gruel

Ingredients:

Sheep liver	60 g
Green Chinese onions	3
Rice	100 g

Process and application:

Remove the membrane from the sheep liver and cut the liver into slices. Cut the green Chinese onions into sections and fry them with the sheep liver in oil in a pan for a moment. Cook rice gruel in another pot until the rice pops off. Then put in the sheep liver and continue heating the gruel until the sheep liver is done. Take the gruel with the sheep liver for breakfast and supper.

Curative properties: Blurring of vision due to old age.

Decoction of Hazelnut Kernel and Wolfberry Fruit

Ingredients:

Hazelnut kernel	50 g
Wolfberry fruit	50 g

Process and application:

Decoct the above ingredients for drinking. Take one decoction each day.

Curative properties: Light-headedness; diminution of vision.

Decoction of Pig Liver and Radish

Ingredients:

Pig liver, radish, fresh ginger slices
and table salt   some for each

Process and application:

Cook the above until the pig liver is done. Take the decoction with the pig liver repeatedly.

Curative properties: Night blindness.

Bitter Gourd Fried in Lard

Ingredients:

Bitter gourd	250 g
Lard	10 g
Green Chinese onion, fresh ginger and table salt	a little for each

Process and application:

Wash the bitter gourd clean, rid it of its seeds and cut it into shreds. Cook the lard until it reaches the 80% of the boiling temperature. Put in the bitter gourd to stir-fry for a moment and season it with flavorings.

Curative properties: Debility; blurring of vision.

Cooked Pig Liver and Chinese Chives

Ingredients:

Pig liver and Chinese chives   some for each

Process and application:

Cook the above in water (unsalted). Eat the soup and the pig liver. This recipe is regularly applicable.

Curative properties: Night blindness in adults and blurring of vision in children.

Hen's Egg White
(for External Application)

Ingredients:

Hen's egg   1

Process and application:

Cook the egg, shell it, stick the hot egg white to the eye-lid (bathed clean) of the patient and bandage it with gauze. Remove the bandage and the egg white the next morning. Apply this for 3 consecutive days.

Curative properties: Conjunctivitis.

Soup of Pig Liver and Spinach

Ingredients:

Pig liver   60 g
Spinach   250 g

Process and application:

Cook soup with the above ingredients and eat the soup twice a day.

Curative properties: Night blindness; this recipe is also helpful in convalescence of sight after infantile measles.

NASAL DISEASES
Powder of Old and Dry Loofahs

Ingredients:
Old and dry loofahs   2
Process and application:
Burn the old and dry loofahs to ash and pound it into powder. Take an infusion of 15 g of the powder in hot water in the morning, once a day.
Curative properties: Nasal carbuncle with turbid nasal discharge.

Sesame Oil

Ingredients:
Sesame oil   some
Process and application:
Put 3 drops of the sesame oil into each nostril at a time, 3 times a day.
Curative properties: Various types of rhinitis.

Sweet Wormwood Decoction

Ingredients:
Sweet wormwood   30 g
Process and application:
Pound it to extract its juice and take the juice with hot water as a drink.
Curative properties: Nosebleed.

Chinese Chives Root with Hen's Egg

Ingredients:

Chinese chives root	120 g
White sugar	30 g
Hen's egg	1

Process and application:

Cook the above ingredients in water until the egg is done. Strain off the liquid, shell the egg and dissolve the white sugar in the liquid. Take the decoction with egg once a day.

Curative properties: Nosebleed.

Thick Soup of Pigskin and Chinese-date

Ingredients:

Pigskin	500 g
Chinese-date	250 g
Crystal sugar	some

Process and application:

Rid the pigskin of the hair and wash it clean, cook it in some water to prepare thick soup. Add the Chinese-date and continue cooking the soup until the pigskin is done. Then add some crystal sugar to it. Take the soup in separate doses with bread or cooked rice.

Curative properties: Nosebleed, gum bleeding due to thrombocytopenia or hemophilia.

DISEASES OF MOUTH CAVITY

Watermelon Juice

Ingredients:

Watermelon   half

Process and application:

Squeeze the watermelon flesh to extract its juice. Keep the juice in mouth and swallow it down after 2 or 3 minutes. Repeat this until all the juice is used.

Curative properties: Aphthous stomatitis; this recipe is also helpful in curing hypertension.

Crystal Sugar Water

Ingredients:

Crystal sugar   100 g

Process and application:

Dissolve the crystal sugar in a bowlful of clear water in a pot and decoct it until half bowl of water is left. Take the water at a draft, twice a day.

Curative properties: Toothache.

Black Soyabean Cooked in Yellow Rice or Millet Wine

Ingredients:

Black soyabean   some
Yellow rice or millet wine   some

Process and application:

Cook the black soyabean in yellow rice or millet wine until the black soyabean is a bit soft. Rinse the mouth with the juice several times.

Curative properties: Toothache; gingival swelling pain.

White Spirit with Prickly-ash Peel

Ingredients:

| Prickly-ash peel | 15 g |
| White spirit | 50 g |

Process and application:

Leave the prickly-ash peel soak in the white spirit for 10 - 15 days, strain the dregs from the white spirit, soak a cotton ball with the white spirit and fill the hole in the dental caries with it to kill the pain. Alternatively, rinse the mouth with this liquid to relieve ordinary toothache.

Curative properties: Toothache due to dental caries; ordinary toothache.

Sesame Oil (as Drops)

Ingredients:

| Sesame oil and salt water | some for each |

Process and application:

Blend dozen drops of sesame oil with one spoonful of salt water. Put 4 - 5 drops of the liquid into the mouth at a time, dozen times a day.

Curative properties: Thrush in children; restlessness.

Pomegranate Extract

Ingredients:

| Fresh pomegranates | 2 |

Process and application:

Remove the seeds of the pomegranates, soak them in hot water, cool the water off and strain off the liquid. Keep the extract in mouth and gargle, several times a day.

Curative properties: Stomatitis; tonsillitis; laryngeal pain; aphthous stomatitis.

Radish Juice

Ingredients:

Radish   some

Process and application:

Wash the radish clean, chop it and pound it to extract its juice. Rinse the mouth with this juice several times a day.

Curative properties: Aphthous stomatitis; stomatocace.

Black Tea

Ingredients:

Black tea   50 g

Process and application:

Decoct the black tea in water, gargle with the tea and then drink the tea, several times a day. Take this continually until the disease is cured. The above dosage is for one dose. Use fresh tea every time.

Curative properties: Dentin hypersensitiveness.

One-clove Garlic *

Ingredients:

One-clove garlic   2 - 3 bulbs

Process and application:

Skin the garlic, roast it over fire and cut it into slices. Apply the hot slices to the pain spot. Renew it when it cools off. Repeat this many times.

Curative properties: Toothache.

---

* One-clove garlic — a var. of garlic (*Bulbus Allii*), bulb of which consists of only one clove.

Hen's Egg White with Burning White Spirit

Ingredients:

White spirit	50 ml
Hen's eggs	2

Process and application:

Beat the eggs to extract the egg white, burn the white spirit in a bowl and pour in the egg white until the fire burns out. Take this recipe when a pain is felt.

Curative properties: Toothache.

Membrane from the Inner Side of the Egg Shell

Ingredients:

Membrane from the inner side of a egg shell   some

Process and application:

Cut a piece of the membrane in the size to the ulcer and soak it in salt water for several minutes. Apply this piece of membrane to the affected area.

Curative properties: Stomatocace.

THROAT DISEASES

Garlic

Ingredients:

Garlic	1 clove
White sugar	1 spoonful

Process and application:

Skin the garlic and remove its big end. Stop the nostril tightly with its thin end. Stop the right nostril if the fish bone sticks at the left side of the throat, and vice versa. At the same time keep sugar in the mouth and swallow it down slowly after it has dissolved in the saliva.

Curative properties: This recipe removes the fish-bone stuck in the throat.

Loofah Powder

Ingredients:

Old loofah   1

Process and application:

Wash the loofah clean, seed it and cut it into small pieces. Decoct it in water for one hour, strain the dregs from the liquid and continue cooking it over slow fire until the decoction becomes somewhat thick, sticky and dry. Remove it from the fire and leave it cool. Mix it with sugar to absorb the liquid, dry it in sun, when dry, pound it into powder and preserve it in a bottle for later use. Take an infusion of 10 g of this powder in hot water as a drink at any time.

Curative properties: Acute pharyngolaryngotracheitis; chronic laryngopharyngitis; tonsillitis.

Tangerine Peel Decoction

Ingredients:

Tangerine peel   250 g

Process and application:

Decoct it for drinking.

Curative properties: Aphonia; sore-throat.

Water Chestnut Extract

Ingredients:

Fresh water chestnut   500 g

Crystal sugar   some

Process and application:
Wash the water chestnut clean, peel it, chop it and wrap it in gauze to squeeze its juice out. Add crystal sugar to the juice and leave it cool. Take 120 ml of the juice at a time, twice a day, for 3 consecutive days.

Curative properties: Acute pharyngolaryngotracheitis; chronic laryngopharyngitis.

Fresh Pear Juice

Ingredients:

Pears	3

Process and application:
Pulp the pears to extract the juice for drinking.

Curative properties: Hoarseness; sore-throat.

Dandelion Herb Decoction

Ingredients:

Dandelion herb	15 g
Peppermint	6 g

Process and application:
Decoct the above ingredients in water and take the decoction as a drink.

Curative properties: Guttural swelling pain; hoarseness; dysphagia.

Cucumber Juice

Ingredients:

Fresh cucumber	500 g
White sugar	30 g

Process and application:
Wash the cucumber clean, peel it, seed it, cut it into

2-cm square cubes, wrap it in gauze and squeeze its juice out. Add sugar and mix it well. Take the juice frequently.
Curative properties: Guttural swelling pain.

Boat-fruited Sterculia Seed Infusion

Ingredients:

Boat-fruited sterculia seed	3 pcs
Honey	15 g

Process and application:
Wash the boat-fruited sterculia seed clean, put it with honey in a tea cup and pour in hot water, cover the cup and leave the boat-fruited sterculia seed infuse in water for 3 - 4 minutes. Take the infusion frequently.
Curative properties: Laryngeal pain; hoarseness.

Loofah Juice (for Oral Administration)

Ingredients:

Fresh loofahs	3

Process and application:
Cut the loofahs into slices and pulp them in a bowl to extract one cup of its juice. Take the juice at a draft.
Curative properties: Laryngitis; tonsillitis; sore-throat.

Decoction of White Radish and Olives

Ingredients:

White radish	1
Olives	10
Crystal sugar	a little

Process and application:
Decoct the above ingredients in water. Take the decoction as a drink, twice a day.

194

Curative properties: Tonsillitis with red swelling.

Black Fungus Powder

Ingredients:

Black fungus   10 g

Process and application:

Roast the black fungus until it is dry and pound it into fine powder, send the powder to the throat by blowing it through a fine tube. The curative effect will be achieved after taking this recipe several times.

Curative properties: Tonsillitis.

Olive Stone Powder

Ingredients:

Olive stone   some

Process and application:

Pound the ingredient into fine powder and take an infusion of the powder in water.

Curative properties: This recipe helps to remove fishbone or chicken-bone stuck in the throat.

Hen's Egg with Honey

Ingredients:

Honey   20 g

Sesame oil   several drops

Hen's egg   1

Process and application:

Beat the egg in a bowl and mix it well. Pour in hot boiling water and add the sesame oil and honey. Take the mixture at a draft, once in the morning and once in the evening on an empty stomach.

Curative properties: Chronic laryngopharyngitis.

Juice of Mangosteen and Olive

Ingredients:

Mangosteen	30 g
Olive	4 pcs
Crystal sugar	50 g

Process and application:

Decoct the mangosteen and olive in water to get 500 - 800 ml of the decoction. Add crystal sugar to the decoction. Take the decoction as a drink, once a day, for 7 consecutive days as a course of treatment.

Curative properties: Chronic laryngopharyngitis; tonsillitis. This recipe can also protect the vocal cords of healthy people.

Mangosteen Powder

Ingredients:

Mangosteen	250 g
White sugar	500 g

Process and application:

Crush the mangosteen and decoct it in water. Strain off the liquid every 30 minutes. Add the same amount of water to decoct and repeat this 3 times. Strain the mixture and combine the 3 decoctions together. Continue heating the decoction over slow fire until it boils down to a sticky substance. Remove it from the fire and leave it cool. Add sugar to absorb the liquid, then dry it in sun. When dry, pound it into powder, preserve this in a bottle for later use. Take an infusion of 10 g powder in hot water at any time.

Curative properties: Acute pharyngitis; chronic pharyngitis; laryngitis.

EAR DISEASES

Bile of a Carp

Ingredients:
Bile of a carp   some
Process and application:
Take out the gallbladder from the carp, squeeze the bile out. Wash out the pus from the ear with hydrogen dioxide solution, put the bile into the ear and stop the ear with a cotton ball, once a day. The disease is to be cured after 3 times of application.

Curative properties: Acute and chronic otitis media.

Loach

Ingredients:
Loach   2
Process and application:
Pulp the loach and apply it to the area around the ear. Renew it once a day, for several consecutive days.

Curative properties: Acute otitis media.

Chinese Chives Juice

Ingredients:
Chinese chives   some
Process and application:
Wash the Chinese chives clean, pound it to extract its juice. Put drops of the juice in the ear with a dropper, 3 times a day.

Curative properties: Chronic supperative otitis media.

Walnut Meat

Ingredients:
Walnut meat   a little
Process and application:
Stew the walnut meat over slow fire. Put the meat in the ear.

Curative properties: Hard earwax.

Rape-seed Oil

Ingredients:
Rape-seed oil   some
Process and application:
Put in 1 - 2 drops of rape-seed oil in the ear to lure out the insect or worm.

Curative properties: This recipe removes an insect or worm that has crept into the ear.

Recipes with Auxiliary Curative Effect for Tumor

NASOPHARYNGEAL CARCINOMA

Purple Gromwell Root Decoction

Ingredients:

Purple gromwell root   30 g

Process and application:

Decoct the above in water. Take one dose each day.

Curative properties: This recipe has auxiliary curative effect on nasopharyngeal carcinoma.

Chinese Chestnut Cake

Ingredients:

Chinese chestnut (uncooked)   500 g

White sugar   250 g

Process and application:

Cook the Chinese chestnut in water for half an hour and when it cools off, peel it. Put it in a bowl and steam it for half an hour. Put it in a container when it is hot, put in sugar, press it into mash with a ladle and mold the mash into cakes. Take the cakes continually.

Curative properties: This recipe has auxiliary curative effect on nosebleed caused by nasopharyngeal carcinoma.

THYROID CANCER

Snake Slough in Hen's Egg

Ingredients:

Snake slough	2 g
Hen's egg	1

Process and application:

Cut a small hole in the egg, put in the snake slough powder through the hole, seal the hole and cook the egg in water. Take one egg at a time, twice a day.

Curative properties: Swelling due to thyroid cancer.

Soup of Pig Pancreas and Dry Mussel

Ingredients:

Pig pancreas	1
Dry mussel	100 - 150 g

Process and application:

Soak the dry mussel in water for 20 minutes and rinse it. Put it with water in an earthenware pot to heat until the water boils. Keep the pot boiling for 10 minutes, put in the pig pancreas and continue cooking them until they are done. Take the soup with seasoning. This recipe can also be taken with bread or cooked rice.

Curative properties: This recipe has auxiliary curative effect on thyroid cancer.

MAMMARY CANCER

Pill of Tortoise Plastron and Dateplum Persimmon

Ingredients:

| Tortoise plastron | several |
| Dateplum persimmon | some |

Process and application:

Parch the tortoise plastron until it becomes yellow, grind it into powder. Stone the dateplum persimmon and pulp it. Mix the above ingredients and roll them into pills. Take 10 g of the pills with hot water each day.

Curative properties: This recipe has auxiliary curative effect on mammary cancer.

Toad Skin

Ingredients:

| Toad skin | 1 |

Process and application:

Apply it to the affected area and renew it once a day.

Curative properties: This recipe kills pain and reduce edema due to mammary cancer.

Jute Leaf

Ingredients:

| Jute leaf | some |

Process and application:

Pulp it and apply it to the affected part. Renew it once every other day.

Curative properties: This recipe is effective on mammary cancer with syndrome of ulcer resistant to healing.

Ointment of Toad

Ingredients:

| Toad | 1 |
| Prickly-ash peel | 200 g |

Vinegar   1000 ml

Process and application:

Boil the above into an ointment. Apply the ointment to the affected part (with a hole left in the center of the ointment).

Curative properties: This recipe kills pain and reduce edema due to mammary cancer.

Decoction of Peel of Green Tangerine and Yellow Rice or Millet Wine

Ingredients:

Peel of green tangerine   15 g
Leaf of green tangerine   15 g
Tangerine seed   15 g

Process and application:

Decoct the above ingredients with yellow rice or millet wine in water for drinking. Take it warm twice a day.

Curative properties: Early stage of mammary cancer.

PULMONARY CARCINOMA

Gallbladders of a Sheep (or of a Pig)

Ingredients:

Gallbladders of a sheep (or pig)   several

Process and application:

Infuse half amount of bile from a gallbladder in water and take it each day, for 7 consecutive days as a course of treatment. Resuming taking it 3 days later.

Curative properties: This recipe has auxiliary curative effect on cough, hemoptysis, expectoration of yellowish sputum and metastasis caused by pulmonary carcinoma.

Toad's Gallbladder

Ingredients:

Toad's gallbladder   dozens

Process and application:

Take bile of 5 toads with water at a time, twice a day. Take this recipe consecutively for 2 months.

Curative properties: This recipe has auxiliary curative effect on cough, hemoptysis, yellowish sputum and metastasis caused by pulmonary carcinoma.

Gruel with Apricot Kernel and Crystal Sugar

Ingredients:

Sweet almond   15 g

Bitter apricot kernel   3 g

Rice   50 g

Crystal sugar   some

Process and application:

Soak the apricot kernel in clear water until they are soft, remove the skin and pound them. Wash the rice clean and soak it until it becomes soft. Cook rice, apricot kernel and crystal sugar in water until they become gruel.

Curative properties: This recipe is effective in relieving asthma due to pulmonary carcinoma.

Gruel with Ginseng and Chinese-dates

Ingredients:

Ginseng   4 - 6 g

Chinese-dates   10

Rice   30 - 60 g

Process and application:

Cook the above ingredients in some water. Take the gruel at a draft or in separate portions. Radish and tea should be avoided.

Curative properties: This recipe has replenishing effect on prostration syndrome and weakness caused by hematorrhea due to pulmonary carcinoma.

Powder of Ginseng and Gecko

Ingredients:

Geckos	2
Ginseng	50 g
White spirit (or honey)	some

Process and application:

Smear white spirit (or honey) on the geckos and roast them until they are done. Grind them along with ginseng into powder. Take an infusion of 4 - 6 g of the powder in warm water, twice a day on an empty stomach.

Curative properties: This recipe produces replenishing effect on phlegm-dyspnea caused by terminal pulmonary carcinoma.

Decoction of Wax-gourd Peel and Broad Bean

Ingredients:

Wax-gourd peel	30 - 60 g
Wax-gourd seed	30 - 60 g
Broad bean	60 g

Process and application:

Decoct the above ingredients in 3 bowlfuls of clear water in a pot until 1 bowl of decoction is left. Strain the decoction and take it. It should be avoided by those who are allergic to broad bean.

Curative properties: This recipe has auxiliary curative

effect on obstinate hydrothorax caused by pulmonary carcinoma.

Stewed Carp with Red Phaseolus Bean

Ingredients:

Red phaseolus bean	90 g
Carp	300 - 500 g

Process and application:

Kill the carp, gut it and wash it clean. Stew it with red phaseolus bean in a deep earthenware pot until they are very soft.

Curative properties: This recipe has auxiliary curative effect in reducing edema caused by pulmonary carcinoma.

Chinese Caterpillar Fungus with Duck Meat (or Lean Pork)

Ingredients:

Chinese caterpillar fungus	10 - 15 g
Duck meat (or lean pork)	some

Process and application:

Steam or stew the above ingredients until they are done. Take them together with the decoction.

Curative properties: This recipe has effect in relieving asthma of those who suffer from hyperhidrosis, dyspnea, cough with dyspnea due to pulmonary carcinoma.

Stewed Chicken with Pseudostellaria Root

Ingredients:

Pseudostellaria root	15 g
Chicken	some

Process and application:

Stew the above together. Take the soup with its contents.

Curative properties: This recipe has auxiliary curative effect on pulmonary carcinoma.

LIVER CANCER

Endive Juice

Ingredients:

Endive	some
White sugar	some

Process and application:

Wash the endive clean, pound it to extract its juice and add sugar to it for oral administration.

Curative properties: This recipe is effective on xerostomia, anorexia due to liver cancer.

House Lizard Soaked in White Spirit

Ingredients:

House lizards (live)	5 - 6
White spirit (with 60% content of alcohol)	500 ml

Process and application:

Soak the house lizard in white spirit in a tin pot or brown glass bottle and keep the pot (or bottle) in dark place for 7 days. Take 10 ml of the liquid at a time, 2 or 3 times a day.

Curative properties: This recipe kills pain caused by liver cancer.

Gruel with Chinese Yam and White Hyaciath Bean

Ingredients:

Chinese yam	30 g
White hyaciath bean	10 g
Rice	100 g

Process and application:

Cook the above ingredients in water until they become gruel.

Curative properties: This recipe is effective on pulmonary carcinoma with diarrhea as the main symptom.

Soup of Water Chestnut

Ingredients:

Meat of water chestnuts	20 - 30

Process and application:

Stew the water chestnut meat in water until the soup turns brown. Eat the soup 2 or 3 times a day.

Curative properties: This recipe has auxiliary curative effect on liver cancer.

Jelly of Eclipta and Fresh Ginger

Ingredients:

Eclipta	500 g
Fresh ginger	30 g
Honey	some

Process and application:

Decoct the eclipta and fresh ginger in water, add honey to the decoction and heat it until it becomes jelly. Take one spoonful of the jelly at a time, 3 times a day.

Curative properties: This recipe has replenishing effect on terminal liver cancer.

CARCINOMA OF ESOPHAGUS

Fresh Chinese Chives Juice

Ingredients:

Fresh Chinese chives   some

Process and application:

Wash the Chinese chives, soak it in hot water and pulp it to extract its juice. Take 100 ml of the juice at a time, 3 times a day.

Curative properties: This recipe has auxiliary curative effect on carcinoma of esophagus.

Fresh Chinese Chives Juice with Milk

Ingredients:

Fresh Chinese chives (or its root)   some
Milk   half a cup

Process and application:

Wash the Chinese chives or its root clean and pound it to extract the juice. Take an infusion of one spoonful of the juice in hot milk at a time (swallow it slowly), several times a day.

Curative properties: This recipe has auxiliary curative effect on carcinoma of esophagus.

Goose Blood

Ingredients:

Fresh goose blood   5 - 10 ml

Process and application:

Draw blood with a syringe from under the wing of the goose and drink the hot blood slowly.

Curative properties: This recipe is effective in removing toxic materials and reducing edema on early stage of carcinoma of esophagus.

Powder of Crucian Carp with Garlic

Ingredients:

Large crucian carp (live)	1
Garlic	some

Process and application:

Gut the crucian carp and descale it. Cut the garlic into thin shreds and use it to stuff the belly of the crucian carp. Wrap the crucian carp in a piece of paper and seal it with a layer of mud. Dry it completely in sun and when dry, roast it in charcoal fire. Remove the mud and paper and pound the fish into fine powder. Take an infusion of 3 g of the powder in rice water at a time, 2 or 3 times a day.

Curative properties: This recipe is effective in removing toxic materials and reducing edema in the early stage of carcinoma of esophagus.

Stewed Pork with Ass-hide Glue

Ingredients:

Ass-hide glue	6 g
Lean pork	100 g

Process and application:

Stew the pork in water first, when the pork is done, put in ass-hide glue and continue stewing the pork until the ass-hide glue dissolves. Season the soup with little table salt and eat the soup with its contents.

Curative properties: This recipe has effect in enriching blood and promoting blood circulation on those who suffer from hemoptysis, asthenia universalis and anemia due to carcinoma of esophagus.

Powder of Chestnut Kernel Skin

Ingredients:

Skin of chestnut kernel   some

Process and application:

Parch it dry and pound it into fine powder. Take an infusion of 3 g powder in warm rice water at a time, 2 or 3 times a day.

Curative properties: Regurgitation, vomiting due to carcinoma of esophagus.

CARCINOMA OF STOMACH

Sophora Flower

Ingredients:

Old sophora flower   10 g
Rice   30 g
Brown sugar   some

Process and application:

Boil rice in water. Add sophora flower to the rice water and take it after dissolving brown sugar in it.

Curative properties: This recipe arrests hematochezia due to carcinoma of stomach.

Decoction of Tangerine Peel and Chinese-date

Ingredients:

Tangerine peel   1
Chinese-dates   3

Process and application:

Stone the Chinese-dates and decoct them with tangerine peel in water. Drink the decoction at short intervals.

Curative properties: Vomiting due to carcinoma of stomach.

Sugarcane Juice Mixed with Fresh Ginger Juice

Ingredients:

Sugarcane and fresh ginger   some for each

Process and application:

Extract half a cup of sugarcane juice and 1 spoonful of fresh ginger juice. Mix them together and stew them for drinking.

Curative properties: This recipe helps to arrest retch and vomiting on the early stage of carcinoma of stomach.

Glutinous Rice Gruel with Ass-hide Glue

Ingredients:

Ass-hide glue	30 g
Glutinous rice	100 g
Brown sugar	a little

Process and application:

Cook glutinous rice gruel. When the gruel is done, put in the ass-hide glue (pounded) and stir the gruel for a moment while heating it.

Curative properties: This recipe has effect in enriching blood and nourishing the stomach on the patients with carcinoma of stomach.

Gruel of Castor Seed Kernel

Ingredients:

| Kernel of castor seed | 20 g |
| Rice | 80 g |

Process and application:
Cook the above ingredients in water for eating.

Curative properties: This recipe has effect in moisturizing instestinal tract and easing constipation due to carcinoma of stomach with symptom of dry stools.

Gruel with Sesame

Ingredients:

Sesame	6 g
Rice	30 g
Honey	some

Process and application:
Roast the sesame in a pan until it smells sweet. Cook rice gruel and when the gruel is nearly done, mix sesame and honey in it.

Curative properties: This recipe has effect in moisturizing intestinal tract and enriching blood on the patient of carcinoma of stomach with symptoms of constipation and hematochezia.

Gruel with Dried Tangerine Peel and Lean Pork

Ingredients:

Dried tangerine peel	9 g
Bone of a cuttlefish	12 g
Lean pork	50 g
Rice	some

Process and application:
Cook rice, dried tangerine peel and bone of a cuttlefish in water until they become gruel. When the gruel is done, fish out the dried tangerine peel and cuttlefish bone,

put in lean pork and continue cooking the gruel. Take the gruel with a little salt as seasoning.

Curative properties: Vomiting due to carcinoma of stomach.

Rice Gruel with Radish Seeds

Ingredients:

Radish seeds	10 - 30 g
Rice	some

Process and application:

Roast the radish seeds and cook them with rice in water.

Curative properties: Abdominal distension caused by carcinoma of stomach.

Boiled Dried Longan Pulp and Peanut Kernels

Ingredients:

Peanut kernels (unskinned)	250 g
Chinese-date	15 g
Dried longan pulp	12 g

Process and application:

Stone the Chinese-date, boil it with peanut kernels and dried longan pulp in water. Take one dose each day.

Curative properties: This recipe has the effect in nourishing the blood on the anemia caused by carcinoma of stomach.

Fried Air Bladder of Fish

Ingredients:

Air bladder of a fish (a large yellow croaker or an

eel)

Process and application:

Fry it in sesame oil until it becomes crisp and crush it. Take an infusion of 10 g of the powder in hot water at a time, 3 times a day.

Curative properties: Gastroptosis and anemia caused by carcinoma of stomach.

INTESTINAL CANCER; ANUS CANCER

Gruel of Water Chestnut

Ingredients:

Water chestnuts	10 - 20
Honey	1 spoonful
Rice	some

Process and application:

Wash the water chestnuts clean and pound it, put them with water in an earthenware pot to cook until the water becomes thick. Add the rice and continue heating them until they become gruel. Put in honey when the gruel is done. Take the gruel at short intervals.

Curative properties: This recipe has effect in moisturizing the intestinal tract on patients of intestinal cancer.

Hen's Egg with Lotus Root Juice and Notoginseng Starch

Ingredients:

Notoginseng starch	3 g
Hen's egg	1
Lotus root juice	some

Process and application:

Mix the lotus root juice with notoginseng starch and

214

put the mixture into the egg through an opening in the shell. Seal the opening with a piece of moist paper and steam the egg until it is done. Take the egg twice a day.

Curative properties: Persistent hematochezia due to intestinal cancer or anus cancer.

Stewed Bananas with Crystal Sugar

Ingredients:

Crystal sugar and bananas   some for each

Process and application:

Peel 1 or 2 bananas and stew them along with some crystal sugar by putting the container in boiling water.

Curative properties: This recipe has auxiliary effect on carcinoma of large intestine.

Decoction of Red-skin Radish* and Water Chestnut

Ingredients:

Red-skin radish and water
    chestnut   equal amount for each

Process and application:

Decoct them and take the decoction as a drink.

Curative properties: This recipe has effect in preventing carcinoma of large intestine and it exerts desirable curative effect on abdominal distension, thirst and anorexia.

---

* Red-skin radish is a var. of *Raphanus sativus* with red skin and white flesh.

Sesame Oil with Spinach

Ingredients:

Fresh spinach and sesame oil   some for each

Process and application:

Wash the spinach clean, soak it in boiling water for 3 minutes and fish it out. Take it after mixing it with sesame oil and seasoning it with flavorings.

Curative properties: This recipe, if taken often, can keep the stool easy; it is also effective in preventing carcinoma of large intestine.

CARCINOMA OF UTERUS

Juice of Sour Pomegranate

Ingredients:

Sour pomegranate   half

Process and application:

Wash it clean and pound it to extract the juice. Take the juice at a draft.

Curative properties: This recipe has effect in astringing the focus and arresting bleeding due to carcinoma of uterus.

Fresh Lotus Root and Biota Tops

Ingredients:

Fresh lotus root   250 g
Biota tops   60 g

Process and application:

Pound them together to extract the juice. Drink the juice with cold boiled water.

216

Curative properties: This recipe has effect in arresting bleeding due to carcinoma of uterus.

Jelly from Scales of a Carp and a Crucian Carp

Ingredients:

Scales of a carp and those of a crucian carp	some for each

Process and application:
Boil the scales over slow fire until they become a jelly. Take an infusion of 30 g of the jelly in warm liquor and water at a time.

Curative properties: This recipe is effective in reducing edema due to carcinoma of uterus.

LEUKEMIA

Beet Juice

Ingredients:

Beet	some

Process and application:
Squeeze the juice out for drinking.

Curative properties: This recipe has auxiliary curative effect on leukemia.

Stewed Eel with Yellow Rice or Millet Wine

Ingredients:

Eel	500 g
Yellow rice or millet wine	500 ml

Process and application:
Gut the eel and wash it clean. Put it in a pot with the wine and clear water to stew over slow fire until the eel is

soft and done. Take it after seasoning it with little salt and soaking it in vinegar.

Curative properties: This recipe is effective in arresting bleeding and replenishing the vital essence on the patients of leukemia with symptoms of hematochezia, leanness and low fever.

Stewed White Jellyfungus with Crystal Sugar

Ingredients:

White jellyfungus	10 - 12 g
Crystal sugar	some

Process and application:

Wash the white jellyfungus clean, soften it by soaking it in cold boiled water for about an hour and rinse the impurities off. Put it in cold boiled water with some crystal sugar in a container and cook it by putting the container in boiling water for 2 - 3 hours. Take the white jellyfungus together with the water.

Curative properties: This recipe is effective in relieving the cough and arresting the bleeding caused by leukemia.

Decoction of Lotus Leaf with Lotus Node Charcoal

Ingredients:

Fresh large lotus leaf	1
Lotus nodes	several

Process and application:

Roast the lotus nodes until they become charcoal and decoct the charcoal along with the lotus leaf in water. Take the decoction at short intervals.

Curative properties: Nosebleed due to leukemia.

Decoction of Chinese-date and Peanut Kernel Skin

Ingredients:

Chinese-date	50 g
Peanut kernels	100 g
Brown granulated sugar	some

Process and application:

Soak the Chinese-date in warm water until it is soft. Cook the peanut kernels in water for a moment, fish them out, leave them cool off and remove the skin for use. Put the Chinese-date and peanut kernel skin in the water that has been used to cook the peanut kernels, add more water and cook them over slow fire for half an hour. Strain the peanut kernel skin from the liquid, put in brown granulated sugar and boil down the decoction.

Curative properties: This recipe is effective in enriching the blood and promoting production of blood for the patients of leukemia or other types of cancer who have abnormal reaction due to radiotherapy and chemotherapy.

Mulberry Syrup

Ingredients:

Fresh mulberry	1000 g (or dried one 500 g)
Honey	300 g

Process and application:

Wash the mulberry clean, decoct it in water and strain off the extract after 30 minutes. Add the same amount of water and continue decocting it. Combine the 2 decoctions together and stew it over slow fire until the decoction becomes thick syrup. Put in honey and continue heating the syrup until it boils. Preserve the syrup in a bottle for later use. Take an infusion of one spoonful of the syrup in hot water at a time, twice a day.

Curative properties: This recipe is effective in nourishing the blood and relieving uneasiness of the mind and body on patients of leukemia.

Soup of Cockcomb Flower and Hen's Egg

Ingredients:

White cockcomb flower	15 - 30 g
Hen's eggs	1 or 2

Process and application:

Decoct the cockcomb flower in 2 bowlfuls of water in a pot until only 1 bowlful of decoction is left. Remove the dregs, beat the egg in the decoction and continue cooking the soup until the egg is done. Take the soup once a day, for 3 - 4 consecutive days.

Curative properties: This recipe arrests bleeding due to leukemia.

Cooked Fleece-flower Root and Hen's Eggs

Ingredients:

Fleece-flower root	6 g
Hen's eggs	2

Process and application:

Cook the above ingredients in water in a deep pot and when they are done, shell the eggs and continue cooking them for a moment. Eat the eggs and drink the decoction.

Curative properties: This recipe has replenishing and nourishing effect on dizziness with dim sight, lassitude in loin and knees, spontaneous perspiration, night sweat due to leukemia.

Glossary

English	Latin	Chinese
areca seed	Semen Arecae	槟榔
argyi leaf	Folium Artemisiae Argyi	艾叶
ass-hide glue	Colla Corii Asini	阿胶
biota tops	Cacumen Biotae	侧柏叶
bitter apricot kernel	Semen Armeniacae Amarum	苦杏仁
bitter gourd	Momordica charantia	苦瓜
black fungus	Auricularia auricula-judae	黑木耳
black sesame seed	Semen Sesami	黑芝麻
black soyabean	Semen Sojae Nigrum	黑豆
black-bone chicken	Gallus Domesticus	乌骨鸡
boat-fruited sterculia seed	Semen Sterculiae Scaphigerae	胖大海
broad bean	Vicia faba	蚕豆
bulb of Chinese onion	Bulbus Allii Fistulosi	大葱白
bulb of green Chinese onion	Bulbus Allii Fistulosi	葱白
carp	Cyprinus carpio	鲤鱼
carrot	Radix Dauci Carotae	胡罗卜
castor-seed	Ricini	蓖麻
celery	Apium graveolens	芹菜
Chinese angelica root	Radix Angelicae Sinensis	当归
Chinese cabbage	Brassica chinensis	油菜
Chinese caterpillar fungus	Cordyceps	冬虫夏草
Chinese chestnut	Castanea mollissmina	板栗
Chinese chive seed	Semen Allii Tuberosi	韭菜籽
Chinese flowering crabapple	Malus spectabilis	海棠
Chinese rose	Flos Rosae Chinensis	月季花
Chinese yam	Rhizoma Diosoreae	山药
Chinese-date	Fructus Ziziphi Jujubae	大枣
Chinese-date	Fructus Ziziphi Jujubae	红枣
chrysanthemum flower	Flos Chrysanthemi	菊花
cockcomb flower	Flos Celosiae Cristatae	鸡冠花

corn	Zea mays	玉米
cuttlefish	inkfish	墨鱼
dandelion herb	Herba Taraxaci	蒲公英
dateplum persimmon	Fructus Diospyri Loti	黑枣
Dragon Well tea	a famous green tea produced in Hangzhou	龙井茶
dried ginger	Rhizoma Zingiberis	干姜
dried tangerine peel	Pericarpium Citri Reticulatae	干橘皮
dry mussel	Mytilus edulis	淡菜
eclipta	Herba Ecliptae	旱莲
endive	Sonchus oleraceus	苦菜
fig	Receptaculum Fici Caricae	无花果
fleece-flower root	Radix Polygoni Multiflori	何首乌
"fragrant mushroom"	Lentinus edodes	香菇
fresh ginger	Rhizoma Zingiberis	生姜
garlic	Bulbus Allii	大蒜
gecko	Gecko (red-spotted house lizard)	蛤蚧
ginger	Zingiber officinale	姜
ginseng	Radix Ginseng	人参
glutinous rice	Semen Oryzae Glutinosae	糯米
green Chinese onion	Allium Fistulosum	葱
green Chinese onion	Allium Fistulosum	大葱
hawthorn fruit	Fructus Crataegi	山楂
honeysuckle flower	Flos Lonicerae	金银花
hyacinth bean	Semen Dolichoris	扁豆
Jew's ear	Auricularia auricula-judae	木耳
laver	Porphyra spp.	紫菜
leaf of Chinese toon	Toona sinensis	香椿
longan aril	Arilus Longan	龙眼肉
lotus leaf	Folium Nelumbinis	荷叶
lotus node	Nodus Nelumbinis Rhizomatis	藕节
lotus plumule	Plumula Nelumbinis	莲心
lotus seed	Semen Nelumbinis	莲子
mallard	Anas platyrhynchos	青头鸭
mallard	Anas platyrhynchos	野鸭
mulberry	Fructus Mori	桑葚(桑椹)
mung bean	Semen Phaseoli Radiati	绿豆

pallas-pit viper	Agkistrodon halys	蝮蛇
paradise fish of China	Cyprinus carpio megalophthalmus	红鲤鱼
peach kernel	Semen Persicae	桃仁
Peking cabbage	Brassica pekinensis	白菜
peppermint	Herba Menthae	薄荷
pickled mustard tuber	Brassica juncea var. tsatsai	榨菜
pilose asiabell root	Radix Codonopsis Pilosulae	党参
pomegranate rind	Pericarpium Grnati	石榴皮
prickly-ash peel	Pericarpium Zanthoxyli	花椒
pseudostellaria root	Radix Pseudostellariae	太子参
pumpkin	Cucurbita	南瓜
purple aubergine	Solanum mebengena var. depresum Bailey	紫茄子
purple gromwell root	Radix Arnebiae seu Lithospermi	紫草根
purslane	Herba Portulacae	马齿苋
radish	Raphanus sativus	罗卜
red bayberry	Myrica rubra	杨梅
red phaseolus bean	Semen Phaseoli	赤小豆
root of American ginseng	Radix Panacis Quinquefolii	西洋参
rose	Flos Rosae Rugosae	玫瑰
sesame oil	Oleum Sesami	麻油
shaddock ped	Pericarpium Citri Grandis	柚皮
silkworm cocoon	Coccum Bombycis	蚕茧
snake slough	Periostracum Serpentis	蛇皮
snow pear	Pyrus serotina Rehd.	雪梨
sophora flower	Flos Sophorae	槐花
spinach	Spinacia oleracea	菠菜
sweet wormwood	Herba Artemisiae	青蒿
talcum powder	Talcum Pulveratum	滑石粉
tangerine seed	Semen Citri Reticulatae	橘核
tomato	Lycopersicum esculentum	番茄
tortoise plastron	Plastrum Testudinis	龟板
tremella	Fungus Tremellae	白木耳
walnut kernel	Semen Juglandis	核桃仁
water chestnut	Eleocharis tuberosa	荸荠
wax-gourd	Benincasa hispida	冬瓜
wax-gourd peel	Exocarpium Benincasae	冬瓜皮

wax-gourd seed	Semen Benincasae	冬瓜籽
white chrysanthemum flower	Flos Chrysanthemi	白菊花
white hyaciath bean	Semen Dolichoris Album; Semen Lablab Album	白扁豆
white jellyfungus	Tremella fuciformis	银耳
white pepper	Fructus Piperisalba	白胡椒
white spirit	(usu. distilled from sorghum or maize)	白酒
wild jujuba seed	Semen Ziziphi Spinosae	酸枣仁
wolfberry fruit	Fructus Lycii	枸杞子
yangtao	Actinidia chinensis	弥猴桃

图书在版编目(CIP)数据

中国食疗:英文/赵慕英编辑 . 温晋根译
– 北京:中国世界语出版社,1996.12
ISBN 7 – 5052 – 0307 – X

Ⅰ. 中… Ⅱ.①赵… ②温… Ⅲ. 食物疗法 – 英文 Ⅳ.R247.1

中国版本图书馆 CIP 数据核字(96)第 11853 号

中国世界语出版社出版
(北京百万庄路 24 号 邮政编码:100037)
北京百花彩印有限公司印刷
中国国际图书贸易总公司发行
(北京车公庄西路 35 号)
北京邮政信箱第 399 号 邮政编码:100044
1996 年第一版第一次印刷
787×1092mm 1/34 7.75 印张
印数 0001 – 5500 册
(英)
ISBN 7 – 5052 – 0307 – X/G·84
02200
14 – E – 2922P